RES

MASONRY

FIREPLACE

AND

CHIMNEY

HANDBOOK

Second Edition

James E. Amrhein, S. E.

Masonry Institute of America

2nd EDITION

Published by

Masonry Institute of America
386 Beech Ave., Suite #4
Torrance, CA 90501-6202
Tel: (310) 328-4400
Fax: (310) 328-4320
www.masonryinstitute.org

Printed in the United States of America

ii

PREFACE

This publication was developed to be simplify and clarify the requirements, design and construction of residential fireplaces and chimneys for use by architects, designers, engineers, building officials, construction inspectors, masons and masonry contractors.

This manual has been prepared to include the requirements of the 1994 Uniform Building Code, Energy Conservation Requirements of the State of California and the U.S. Department of Housing and Urban Development.

ACKNOWLEDGEMENTS

The construction suggestions and recommendations offered by Ben and Angelo Cassara are gratefully acknowledged. Their able assistance helped make this book a practical and useful publication.

The information and details furnished by Superior Fireplace Company and Whittier Steel & Manufacturing, Inc. are appreciated.

We appreciate the information provided by James Buckley on Rumford fireplaces. The suggestions and assistance of Scott McNear are acknowledged. Thomas Escobar, architect, prepared the drawings and page make up. Petra Stadtfeld did the typing and computer desk top typesetting for this publication, Michele Amrhein and Kristine Kaligian assisted in the proofreading.

MASONRY INSTITUTE OF AMERICA

The Masonry Institute of America, founded in 1957 under the name of Masonry Research, is a promotional, technical research organization established to improve and extend the use of masonry. Supported by the mason contractors through a labor management contract between the unions and contractors, the Masonry Institute of America is active in Southern California in promoting new ideas and masonry work, improving building codes, conducting research projects, presenting design, construction and inspection seminars and writing technical and non-technical papers, all for the purpose of improving the masonry industry.

INTERNATIONAL CONFERENCE OF BUILDING OFFICIALS (ICBO)

TABLE OF CONTENTS

A fireplace gives warmth and beauty to a home

GENERAL

1.1   *Introduction*

For thousands of years fire has been a focal point of human existence. Fire offers warmth in cold weather, cooks the food we eat, provides light in darkness and fireplaces serve as social gathering points for friends and families.

Modern technology challenges the need for and use of traditional fireplaces. At one time it was the center of activity in the kitchen as the only means of cooking, but now, the fireplace is in the living room or family room. Traditional flame-cooking methods are maintained by use of the barbecue, an evolutionary form of the fireplace.

The usefulness of a fire's warmth is a factor in the fireplace in the family room which once was the primary heat source for the entire house, until replaced by newer heating systems, such as forced air heating widely used today.

Despite these shifts away from being a necessity in a home, fireplaces retain an important part of most current popular construction designs. Enhancements such as gas log lighters and glass fireplace screens has integrated the traditional fireplace into the modern residence. A functional fireplace makes a house into a home, as it is difficult to imagine warming up to a forced-air outlet or a clanking radiator in the same manner as cozying up to the amiable warmth of a hearth.

Fireplaces and chimneys are important elements in the design and construction of a home. Whether in the living room or recreation room, the fireplace in the home is a central feature around which to entertain friends and enjoy good times.

The chimney can be a dominant, interesting architectural feature on the exterior of a home, an attractive element of a architectural design. As such, a well-designed home needs a fireplace and chimney that are aesthetically and architecturally pleasing as well as effective and energy efficient.

The well designed fireplace not only adds to the beauty of a home, but it also adds an interest while in use. The features and requirements of fireplace design set forth in this publication have been proven and used successfully for years and are essential for proper fireplace and chimney performance.

1.2 How Does a Fireplace and Chimney Work?

Why does a log burn better in a fireplace than in an open field? How does a fireplace and chimney work to provide good burning and a satisfactory fire?

There are several reasons fireplaces burn fuel well:

1. Fuel (wood log) is placed in the firebox on a grate to permit air to flow under and around it. It is then ignited by means of a gas log lighter or match struck under paper or kindling wood. Combustion continues as long as air is supplied, but not to such an extent that the fire is blown out. This requires a controlled air flow.

2.   The air flow is controlled by means of the fireplace opening, the damper and the flue.

3.   At start-up, the average temperature of the air in the chimney is relatively low; consequently the draft or upward air flow is also low, some combustion products (i.e. gases and smoke) may spill into the room until the chimney has become warm enough to raise the average temperature of the gas has increased to produce a sufficient draft.

4.   As the fuel continues to burn, the products of combustion rise into the throat of the chimney through the damper and into the smoke chamber. As the heated air, gas and smoke rise fresh air is sucked into the fire. This continuous supply of fresh air is provided by an outside air intake.

5.   The smoke and gases expand through the throat and into the smoke chamber and rise up through the flue.

6.   The fireplace heats the room by radiating the heat from the fire with the sloped or curved back and angled sides of the firebox. The heat continues to radiate from the masonry long after the fire has been extinguished.

7.   Each of the following elements—fireplace opening, throat, damper, smoke chamber, flue and chimney—is important in contributing to well-performing fireplaces.

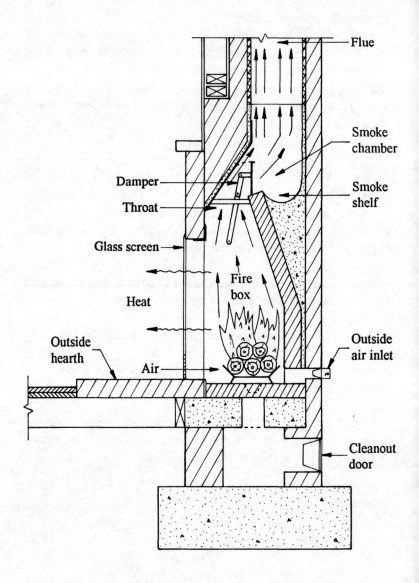

Figure 1-1   Air and heat flow in a fireplace and chimney

FIREPLACES

2.1   Types of Fireplaces

2.1.1   Single Face — There are several types of fireplaces used in residential construction. The most frequently used is the single face fireplace (Figure 2-1). This is a fireplace in which the firebox faces the room and is in the same plane as the wall.

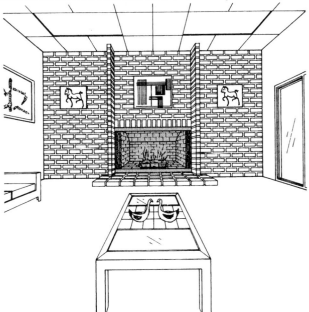

Figure 2-1   Single face fireplace

2.1.2 *Multiple Face* — Another type is the multi-face fireplace (Figures 2-2, 2-3, 2-4 and 2-5), in which two or three faces are open to one or two rooms. Special consideration must be given to draft through proper flue size for this type of fireplace.

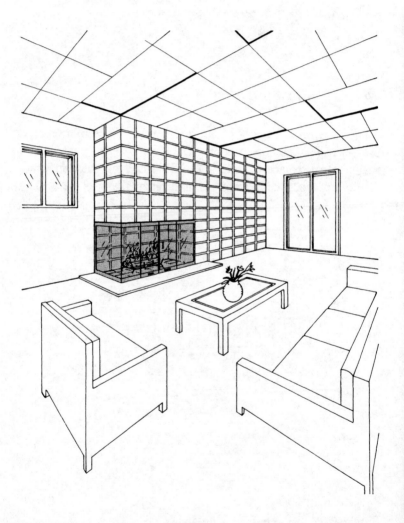

Figure 2-2 **L shaped fireplace**

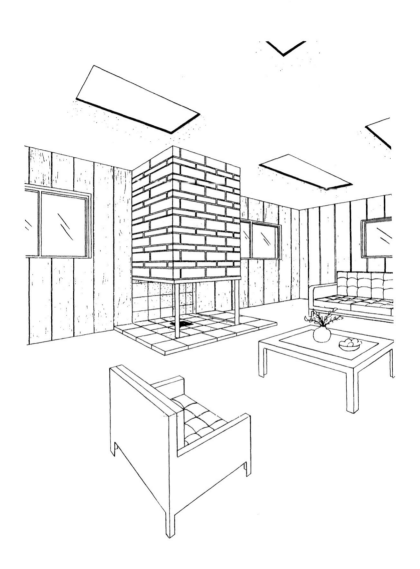

Figure 2-3   Three face fireplace (long front, short sides)

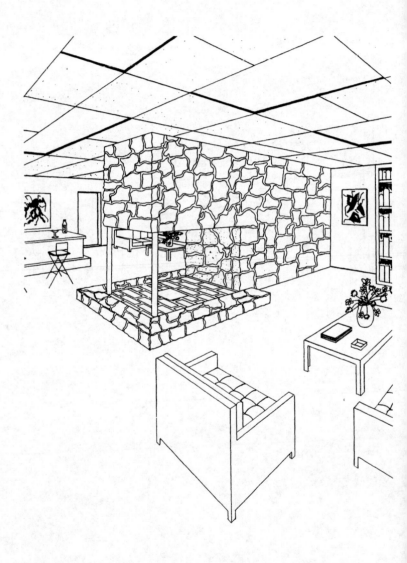

Figure 2-4   Three face fireplace (short front, long sides)

Figure 2-5   See-thru or double view fireplace

2.1.3 *Corner Fireplace* — Quite frequently rooms lend themselves to locating fireplaces in a corner (Figure 2-6), and this will enhance that particular area of the room   The configuration shown in Figure 2-7 is a corner fireplace and an adjacent barbecue with one chimney, but each one must have its own flue.

Figure 2-6   Corner fireplace

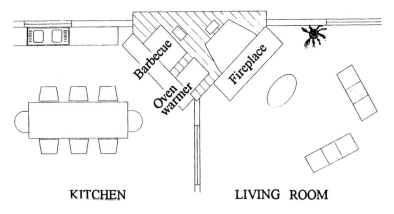

Figure 2-7   Combined corner fireplace and barbecue

2.1.4   Fireplaces on Opposite Sides of Wall — Many times it is convenient to place fireplaces adjacent to each other but facing into opposite rooms, as shown in Figure 2-8. This can be either for adjacent living rooms in an apartment building or for an indoor-outdoor fireplace arrangement in which one fireplace can serve as a barbecue or fireplace on the porch or patio and the other may be in the living room or playroom. The fireplace may also serve as a separation between rooms such as a living room and a den or a playroom. This sketch shows a staggered position for each fireplace with each fireplace having its own flue.

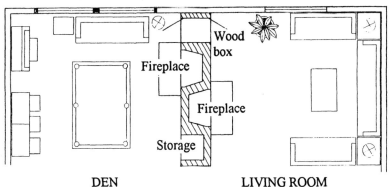

Figure 2-8   Fireplaces on opposite sides of wall

2.1.5 *Unusual Design* — In addition to single face fireplaces and multi-face fireplaces, there are fireplaces of unusual configurations, such as round fireplaces (Figure 2-9), completely freestanding fireplaces, and multiple fireplaces that face more than one room.

An abundance of fireplace designs exist; however, they each must follow the basic principles of good design to insure satisfactory burning conditions without smoking.
It is strongly recommended that odd shaped fireplaces be avoided. Special precautions may have to be taken to prevent smoking that may make such fireplaces too costly or less than satisfactory.

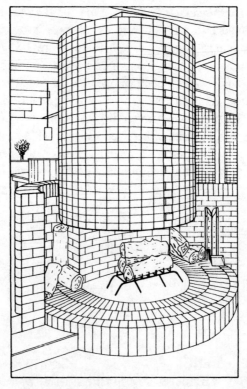

Figure 2-9   Round fireplace

2.1.6   *The Rumford Fireplace* — Count Rumford, for whom this type of fireplace is named, was born Benjamin Thompson in Woburn, Massachusetts in 1753. He spent much of his life as an employee of the Bavarian government where he received his title, "Count of the Holy Roman Empire." Rumford is known primarily for his work on the nature of heat. He discovered that heat was transferred "by conduction, convection or radiation."

In 1796, Count Rumford set forth the principles for the construction of an efficient fireplace. Rumford's study of the fireplace based on the concept of radiation. He recognized that fire radiates heat waves from the fireplace to various objects in the room, thereby heating them, so he used brick and flat stones rather than rubble stones to reflect the heat more effectively. It is likely that he was the very first scientist to consider the heating properties of radiation.

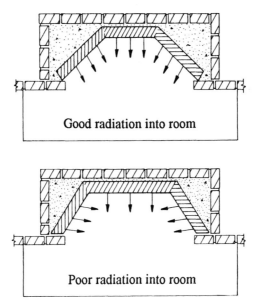

Figure 2-10   **The radiation of heat was aided when the sides and back were slightly angled or curved from the back to the front**

Rumford stated that "The best fireplace is not deep and squatty, but shallow and high with slanted sides and back."

Rumford improved the fireplaces of his day by making them more shallow with widely angled covings to reflect more heat into the room. He streamlined the throats of his fireplaces so they would draw without smoking and with a minimal loss of heated room air. (See Figure 2-11). His fireplaces had straight backs and rounded throats, as shown in the drawing published in his first essay on fireplaces in 1796.

Rumford fireplaces were all the rage in America right after his essay appeared. But in America many, including Thomas Jefferson, who had Rumford fireplaces built at Monticello, thought the fireplace should be a little deeper so bigger logs could be burned in them. To make the fireboxes deeper at the hearth they sometimes sloped the fireback which was also believed to reflect more heat into the room. Rumford himself contributed to this idea in his first essay, "Practical Directions .... for Workmen."

In a footnote about a special case, he indicated he had made a very small fireplace a little deeper by slanting the back wall of the firebox a few inches back right over the fire.

If he had kept the fireback vertical in this instance, it would have only been about eight inches (203 mm) deep. Rumford thought it should be about twelve inches (305 mm) deep to be big enough to maintain a fire. He said that this particular small fireplace seemed to be an especially good heater and he wasn't sure why, speculating it was the additional radiation off the slanted back wall.

Whether valid or not, Rumford only slanted the back - actually made more of a niche or pocket for a firebasket - on this one very small fireplace out of the five or six hundred fireplaces he "improved." It would, therefore, be incorrect to say Rumford advocated fireplaces with slanted firebacks - especially fireplaces with slanted backs and without streamlined throats. Rumford repeated in his second essay on fireplaces, published in 1798, that it is very important to "round off the breast ..." and later in the same essay he characterized sloping firebacks as a "mistake."

Rumford was also aware of smoke and the flow of gases and recognized certain principles had to be followed to convey the smoke away from the fire, allow proper air for combustion and create a proper throat to assist in the flow of gases. Today, fireplaces are relatively small and fairly deep and thus the full benefit of the fire's radiation into the room is not realized.

2.1.6.1   Rumford Basic Principles

The basic principles of the heat-radiating Rumford fireplace are as follows:

1.   The fireplace opening is essentially square, roughly as tall as it is wide.

2.   The depth is between one third and one half of the width of the fireplace opening so that a three foot (914 mm) wide Rumford would be between twelve inches (305 mm) and eighteen inches (457 mm) deep.

3.   The fireback is about the same dimension as the depth and the covings, or sides of the firebox, are angled at from 45° to 60° to the face depending on the depth.

4.   The fireback is straight and plumb, as shown in Rumford's original 1796 plate (Figure 2-11), although there is a common variation in which the fireback gently slopes or curves forward after rising vertically from hearth for about the same dimension as the fireplace depth (Figure 2-15).

5.   The throat of a Rumford fireplace is very small, typically about four inches (102 mm) deep and as wide as the fireback – as little as one twentieth of the area of the fireplace opening. The throat, which is in front of the smoke shelf, usually has a damper that controls the smoke and air flow. Rumford insisted the throat be rounded and streamlined to prevent the fireplace from smoking, but many masons have neglected this streamlining.

Rumford fireplace designed and built by James Buckley Photo by Lou Coopey

2.1.6.2   Rumford Design

Rumford's fireplace recommendations are for a wide, high fireplace with a relatively shallow interior hearth.

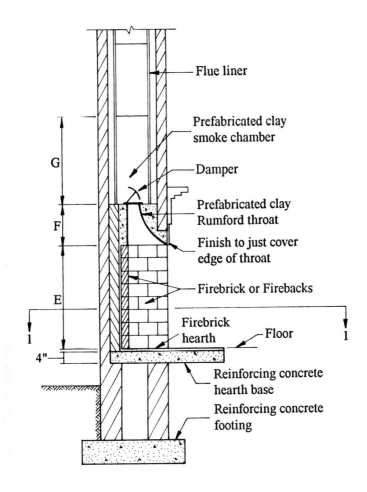

Figure 2-11   Cross-section based on the original Rumford fireplace design with prefabricated clay throat and smoke chamber

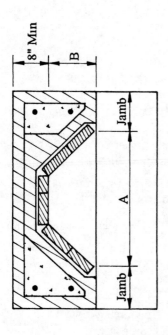

SECTION 1-1

Figure 2-12   Cross-section thru the fire box of a Rumford fireplace

Table 2-A — Rumford Fireplace Dimensions*

Fireplace Size wide	Throat A x F	Dampers Frame	Smoke Chamber (Base x G)	Flue Tile	Other dimensions: A	B	C	D	E	F	G
24"	24"x12"	4"x16"	8.5"x18"x24"	8.5"x13"	24"	12"	13.5"	13.5"	24"-28"	12"	24"
30"	30"x12"	9"x24"	13"x27"x30	13"x13"	30"	12"	13.5"	15"	28"-32"	12"	30"
36"	36"x14"	9"x24"	13"x27"x30	13"x13"	36"	14"	13.5"	18"	32"-38"	14"	30"
42"	42"X15"	9"x30"	13"x34"x30	13"x18"	42"	15"	15"	21"	38"-42"	15"	30"
48"	48"x16"	9"x30"	16"x34"x30	16"x20"	48"	16"	18"	22.5"	42"-48"	16"	30"

*For metric dimensions in millimeters multiply by 25.4

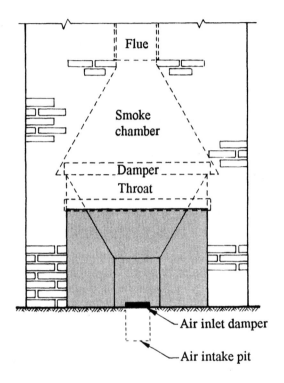

Figure 2-13   Elevation of Rumford fireplace showing damper and smoke chamber with a centered flue

2.1.6.3   *Modified Rumford Design*

It was during the early 1800's that the slant-backed Rumford variation was popularized, as described in Vrest Orton's book "The Forgotten Art of Building a Good Fireplace", Yankee Press, 1969.

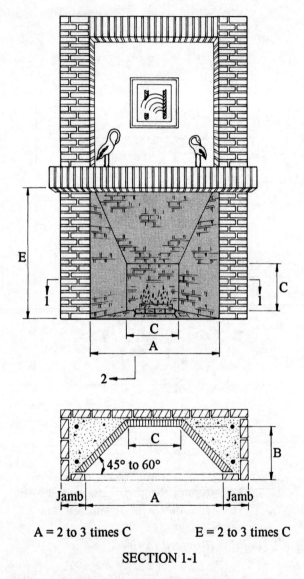

A = 2 to 3 times C   E = 2 to 3 times C

SECTION 1-1

For dimensions see Table 2-A

Figure 2-14   Elevation and cross-section of modified Rumford fireplace

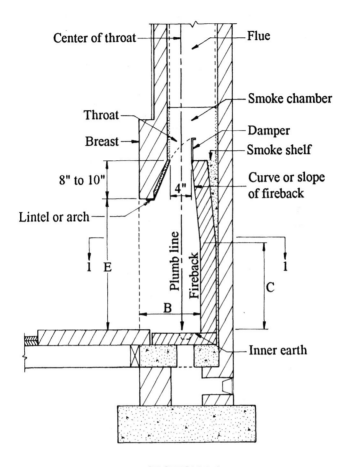

Center of throat — Flue

Throat

Breast

Smoke chamber

Damper

Smoke shelf

Curve or slope of fireback

8" to 10"

4"

Lintel or arch

Plumb line

Fireback

E

B

C

Inner earth

SECTION 2-2

Figure 2-15   Cross-sectional side elevation of a modified Rumford fireplace and chimney as described by Vrest Orton

The size of the flue directly above the smoke chamber should be $1/10$ the size of the fireplace opening; thus if the fireplace opening is 40 inches (1016 mm) wide by 60 inches (1524 mm) high, an area of 2400 square inches (1.55 m²), the flue should have an area of 240 square inches (0.155 m²).

Rumford recommended that the chimney should be a sufficient height to clear the roof and to be two to three feet (0.6 to 0.9 m) above all surrounding obstructions such as a roof ridge, dormer windows, nearby trees and surrounding buildings.

If there are high winds that could blow into the chimney and cause the fireplace to smoke, a deflector or cone should be placed on top of the chimney to prevent the wind from blowing down the chimney.

These recommendations by Sir Benjamin, known as Count Rumford, have been used for 200 years and have resulted in smokeless, heat-generating efficient fireplaces.

The details and dimensions of the Rumford Fireplace are courtesy of the Superior Clay Corp., P.O. Box 352, Uhrichsville, OH 44683, and Technical Services provided by James Buckley of the Buckley Rumford Co., P.O. Box 2712, Seattle, WA 98111.

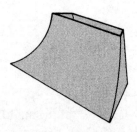

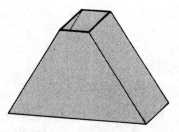

Figure 2-16 Prefabricated clay throat for Rumford fireplace 20", 30", 36", 42" and 48" wide

Figure 2-17 Prefabricated clay smoke chamber

2.2   Fire Pits

In garden rooms, large dens, cocktail lounges and restaurants, central firepits with hoods are attractions that invite everyone to sit around them. The fire pit, Figure 2-18, should be lined with fire brick and the exterior wall may be made of various types of stone, brick or block masonry.

Figure 2-18   Fire pit with hood

2.3   Barbecues

Barbecues may be constructed with or without curved firebacks or smoke shelves provided the fire pit on the open sides is surrounded by solid brick masonry or 16-gauge (1.61 mm) metal, the top of which should be not less than 30 inches (762 mm) above the adjacent floor level, and provided that the floor of the barbecue pit is depressed, not less than six inches (152 mm) below the surrounding masonry or metal lip. No more than two sides of the firebox may be open. In the above type of construction hearth slab is not required for barbecues.

Figure 2-19   Combination barbecue and fireplace

2.4   Framing the Fireplace Opening

Many times it is desirable to provide more than a flat face on the fireplace. This can be done by protruding or corbeling masonry units out from the face of the fireplace (Figures 2-20 and 2-21) or changing its shape from a rectangle. A projecting brick edge will emphasize the fireplace opening.

Figure 2-20   Raised firebox with framed opening

By use of an arch (Figure 2-21), the shape is changed and it is possible to eliminate the steel lintel angle.

Figure 2-21   Fireplace opening with an arch

2.5   *Parts of a Fireplace and Chimney*

Anchors: Anchors are straps of steel that are secured into the bond beam and are tied back to the floor joists, roof rafters or wall members. The anchors tie the chimney to the house, which may provide support in the event of wind or earthquake.

Ash Dump: The trap door on the floor of the inner hearth that leads to the ash pit.

Ash Pit: The ash pit is the space into which the ashes are dumped. It is a non-combustible storage compartment behind or below the firebox, which helps keep the fireplace clean without having to carry ashes through the house.

Bond Beam: A bond beam is a member poured in the masonry at the support level of the chimney. The support level is usually at the floor and at the ceiling or roof line. It may also be above the roof line if the chimney is tall enough to require a supplementary support.

Chimney (Fireplace): A shaft built to carry off smoke and products of combustion that extends from the top of the throat of the fireplace to the top or cap of the chimney.

Chimney Breast: The area above the lintel or opening and in front of the throat, also called the fireplace face.

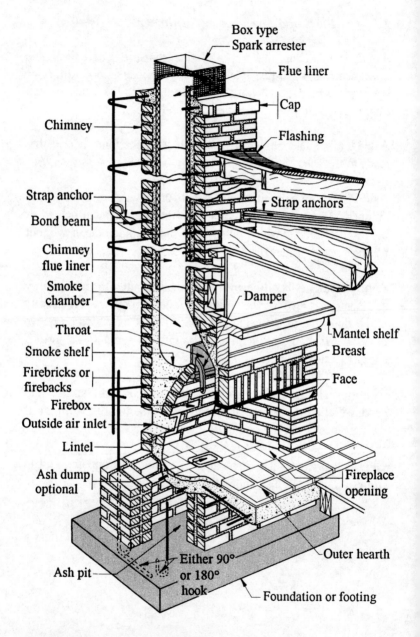

Figure 2-22 Parts of a fireplace and chimney

Chimney Cap: Chimneys should always be designed with a sloping cap to prevent water from running down next to the flue lining and into the fireplace. The chimney cap also prohibits water from standing at the top and creating frost or moisture problems. The chimney cap prevents the brick and masonry of the chimney from becoming soaked from the top down. The chimney flue liners should project approximately two inches (51 mm) to four inches (102 mm) above the highest point of the chimney cap.

Chimney Flue: Smoke and combustion gases from the fire pass up the chimney inside the flue. Each fireplace should have an independent flue, entirely free from other openings or connections. A flue may be lined or unlined. An unlined chimney flue should be larger than a lined chimney flue. The proper sizes of chimney flues may be seen in Tables 2-B and 2-C. The size of the flue and the height of the chimney above the roof are important to create the proper draft through the fireplace and to insure adequate burning of fuel and passage of smoke. It is important to obtain a positive and uniform draft over the full width of the fireplace. The flue lining should be supported on at least three sides by a ledge of projecting mortar, brick or masonry, finishing flush with the inside of the lining. Supporting masonry should not project past the inside of the lining.

Chimney Hood: A chimney hood is an extension or baffle on the top of the chimney or flue lining that diverts wind currents away from the chimney opening, prevents downdrafts and improves the draft of the chimney.

Chimney Flue Lining: Chimney flue linings are fire clay, terra cotta, concrete pumice or other approved material made to be installed inside a chimney. Liners begin at the top of a smoke chamber. Clay flue linings must conform to ASTM C-315. When chimney design requires the flues to angle, the flues should not slope more than 30° from the vertical.

Concrete pumice flue linings such as Hi-Temp® flue lining by Graystone Block Co. conform to ICBO Evaluation Report No. 2602 and UL Standard 1777 or Supaflu chimney lining, ICBO Evaluation Report No. 3937.

Chimney Top or Chimney Pot: A chimney top is a clay or concrete extension to the flue that adds height and provides a decorative top to the chimney.

Damper: Dampers are required on all chimneys and should be placed at the forward part of the masonry fireplace, immediately in back of the breast wall of the fireplace and in the throat of the firebox. They should be properly sized and extend the full width of the throat to regulate the draft and air passing from the firebox into the smoke chamber. The damper also reduces loss of heat up the chimney and can be closed when the fireplace is not in use. The damper can also be used to regulate the rate of burning in the firebox.

Exhaust Fan: An exhaust fan is a mechanical fan that increases the draft through the flue and prevents smoking and backdrafts.

Fire Brick: Fire brick is a hard-fired refractory brick that may line a firebox and is able to resist the heat of a fire. A fireplace lined with fire brick will help reduce maintenance of the firebox.

Firebox, Combustion Chamber or Firepot: The chamber, or area where the fire is built, is the firebox. It generally is built with fire brick laid with thin joints. The side walls are slanted slightly to radiate heat into the room. The rear wall is sloped or curved to provide an upward draft action into the throat above the firebox, so combustion gases may exit up the chimney.

Fireplace Hood: A hood is an ornamental fixture of masonry or metal that is sometimes placed in front of and above the fireplace opening. (See UBC Sec. 3102.7.4 - page 196).

Fireplace Opening: The fireplace opening is the area between the side face and the lintel. It is the opening into the firebox in which the fire is built. The area of the fireplace opening governs the flue size.

Flashing: Flashing is sheet metal between the chimney and the roof, embedded into the chimney and under the roofing material to prevent rain from leaking between the roof and the chimney.

Footing: The footing should consist of concrete at least twelve inches (305 mm) thick and should extend at least six inches (152 mm) beyond the foundation walls on all sides.

Foundation: The foundation of a chimney is usually made of masonry or poured concrete designed to support the weight of the chimney, resist frost action on the structure or any additional load imposed and to prevent the settling or tipping of the chimney. The foundation generally is unreinforced, with only the chimney reinforcing bars extending from it when required. Most codes require the foundation to be at least eight inches (203 mm) thick.

Gas Log: A gas log is a self-contained, free-standing, open-flame, gas-burning appliance consisting of a metal frame or base supporting simulated logs and designed for installation only in a vented place.

Hearth: The hearth is the floor of the fireplace. There is both an inner hearth and an outer hearth. The inner hearth may be made of fire-resistant brick and holds the burning logs; the outer hearth may be of brick, tile or other noncombustible building products. It is supported on concrete or may be part of the concrete slab.

Lintel: The lintel is the member above the fireplace opening that supports the decorative face or breast of the fireplace. The lintel may be a steel angle or may be reinforced masonry. In some designs it may be incorporated into the damper assembly.

Mantel Shelf: A mantel shelf is above the fireplace opening that serves as a decorative device to hold ornaments. The mantel may be made of wood, masonry, marble or other material.

Outside Air Inlet: This is an energy conservation feature and is required for fireplaces located on an exterior wall. It is intended to reduce the amount of preheated room air used for combustion.

Smoke Chamber: The smoke chamber acts as a funnel to compress the smoke and gases from the fire so that they will squeeze into the chimney flue above. The smoke chamber is important for good draft action. It should be symmetrical in shape so that the draft pulls evenly on the fire in the firebox. A symmetrical smoke chamber prevents a fire from burning on one side or the other of the firebox, causing eccentric flame action. The smoke chamber should be centered with the flue directly above the fireplace and its walls should be sloped at the same angle to provide even draft from the firebox to the chimney. A smoke chamber also has a smoke shelf to catch soot and thus provides a cleaner fireplace.

Smoke Shelf: A smoke shelf is located at the bottom of the smoke chamber behind the damper and can collect soot and also gather any rain water that runs down the chimney. A smoke shelf improves draft conditions in a chimney and help eliminate downdrafts.

Spark Arrester: The spark arrester is a screen on top of the flue that prevents sparks or other combustible material from blowing out the chimney and igniting brush, wooded areas and even roof tops. Spark arresters are recommended for all fireplaces and are required in brush, forest and national park areas and in many jurisdictions. The spark arrester is of corrosion resistant wire mesh with openings not larger than ½ inch square (162 mm²).

Throat: The throat is a slot-like opening directly above the firebox through which flames, smoke and combustion gases pass into the smoke chamber. It is usually fitted with a damper.

2.6   Fireplace Location

When considering the location of the fireplace, thought should be given to the traffic pattern, the placement of the furniture in relation to the exits, and the gathering area in front of the fireplace. Attempts should be made to locate a fireplace so there will not be a path of traffic too close to the fireplace.

Ideally, the fireplace should be located on the interior of the building so that no heat will be lost to the outside.

The warm air outlet register of a forced air furnace should never be located near a fireplace, especially in cases where a draft would be created across the front of the fireplace. Such a draft would create a downdraft, with the result that smoke could enter the room. Should such a location be necessary, a register with vanes to direct the air upward should be used.

A fireplace should never be located across the room from an outside door, because when the door is open, a gust of wind could blow smoke or sparks from the fireplace into the room.

2.7   Size of Fireplace

Careful consideration should be given to the size of the fireplace as it relates to the room in which it is to be located. This is important not only for the fireplace's appearance, but for its operation as well. If too small, the fireplace will not produce a sufficient amount of heat, even though it functions properly. If too large, a fire that fills the combustion chamber would be entirely too hot for the room. Also, a small fire in a large fireplace does not provide an aesthetically pleasing appearance.

Moreover, a large fireplace requires a larger chimney and flue and could, therefore, require an abnormal amount of air supply for combustion. When a large fireplace and flue are used, gas lighters should be installed to heat up the flue air slowly and smokelessly. This will heat the air and start a satisfactory draft necessary for good combustion of the wood logs and thus prevent smoke from entering the room.

A fireplace opening should be approximately $1/30$ to $1/65$ of the room area, with the $1/30$ ratio applying to small rooms and $1/65$ ratio to large rooms. Table 2-B gives suggested widths of the Fireplaces appropriate to room sizes.

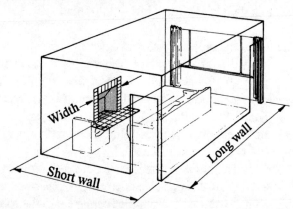

Figure 2-23   Width of fireplace

The height-to-width ratio can vary considerably, depending upon design, wall size, location, etc., but is generally between 1:1 and 1:2. A minimum size fireplace opening would be approximately 24 inches (610 mm) high by 24 inches (610 mm) wide.

Table 2-B — Suggested Width of Fireplace Openings
Appropriate to Size of Room

Size of Room in Feet (Meters)	Width of Fireplace Opening in inches (mm)	
	If in Short Wall	If in Long Wall
Feet (Meters)	Inches (mm)	Inches (mm)
10 x 14 (3.0 x 4.3)	24 (610)	24 to 32 (610 to 813)
12 x 16 (3.7 x 4.9)	28 to 26 (711 to 914)	32 to 36 (813 to 914)
12 x 20 (3.7 x 6.1)	32 to 36 (813 to 914)	36 to 40 (914 to 1016)
12 x 24 (3.7 x 7.3)	32 to 36 (813 to 1016)	36 to 48 (914 to 1219)
14 x 28 (4.3 x 8.5)	32 to 40 (813 to 1016)	40 to 48 (1016 to 1219)
16 x 30 (4.9 x 9.1)	30 to 40 (762 to 1016)	48 to 60 (1219 to 1524)
20 x 36 (6.1 x 11.0)	40 to 48 (1016 to 1219)	48 to 72 (1219 to 1829)

The ideal dimensions of a single-face fireplace have been determined by experience to be 36 inches (914 mm) wide by 26 inches (660 mm) high by 20 inches (508 mm) deep. If the height of the fireplace is increased, the depth of the firebox should be increased in the same proportion for the ideal dimensions.

Example: A fireplace 32 inches (813 mm) high should have a depth of:

20 inches x $(^{32}/_{26})$ = 25 inches

$(508$ x $(^{813}/_{660}) = 626$ mm).

It is important to provide sufficient depth so that smoke and fire will not discolor and blacken the breast or front of the fireplace.

Fireplace openings should not be too high, for the usual width of the opening the height above the hearth is seldom more than 32 inches (813 mm). Table 2-C give the widths, heights and depths of fireplace openings found to be most satisfactory for appearance and efficient operation in residential construction. These dimensions may be varied to meet the module of the brick or to fit any special dimensions of the room area.

Table 2-C   Fireplace Dimensions

Fireplace Type	Width of opening W.		Height of opening H.		Depth of opening D.	
	(in.)	(mm)	(in.)	(mm)	(in.)	(mm)
Single Face	28	(711)	24	(610)	20	(508)
	30	(762)	24	(610)	20	(508)
	30	(762)	26	(660)	20	(508)
	36	(914)	26	(660)	20	(508)
	36	(914)	28	(711)	22	(559)
	40	(1016)	28	(711)	22	(559)
	48	(1219)	32	(813)	25	(635)
Two Face adjacent "L" or corner Type	34	(864)	27	(686)	23	(584)
	39	(991)	27	(686)	23	(584)
	46	(1168)	27	(686)	23	(584)
	52	(1321)	30	(762)	27	(686)
Two Face* opposite Look thru	32	(813)	21	(533)	30	(762)
	35	(889)	21	(533)	30	(762)
	42	(1067)	21	(533)	30	(762)
	48	(1219)	21	(533)	34	(864)
Three Face* 2 long, 1 short 3 way opening	39	(991)	21	(533)	30	(762)
	46	(1168)	21	(533)	30	(762)
	52	(1321)	21	(533)	34	(864)
Three Face* 1 long, 2 short 2 way opening	43	(1092)	27	(686)	23	(584)
	50	(1270)	27	(686)	23	(584)
	56	(1422)	30	(762)	27	(686)

*NOTE: Fireplaces that open on more than one front and one end are NOT recommended.

2.8   *Flush or Raised Hearth*

The hearth is the floor of the firebox and the area in front of it. It protects the wood floor or carpet of the room from sparks and ashes. Floor level or flush hearths may spread over a large area to create an in-the-room fireplace feeling, or they may be depressed to permit sitting steps around the fireplace.

A raised hearth (Figure 2-24) elevates the fire to a comfortable viewing level; it also creates an intimate atmosphere and is well proportioned for a small room. Raised hearths may be built up from the floor and extended out to each side to allow for seating room. There are requirements for the minimum depth of hearth extensions but not on maximum extensions.

Figure 2-24   Fireplace with a raised hearth

A feeling of a floating hearth can be achieved by cantilevering the raised outer hearth over the floor. The smooth flow of the floor under the hearth platform expands the room and creates a feeling of spaciousness. A cantilevered hearth should be reinforced concrete and can be covered with stone, brick or other non-combustible materials.

For fireplaces up to six square feet ($0.6m^2$), or with an opening of approximately three feet (914 mm) by two feet (610 mm), the hearth extension must be 16 inches (406 mm) out from the front of the fireplace and eight inches (203 mm) beyond the sides of the fireplace opening. For larger-sized fireplaces, these dimensions increase to 20 inches (508 mm) from the front to twelve inches (305 mm) from the side.

The extended hearth must be made of completely non-combustible materials; brick or stone are most popular.

2.9   Lintel

The lintel is a structural member over the fireplace opening that supports the masonry. It may be a steel angle, in which case provision should be made for expansion by wrapping the ends with fiberglass wool or some other means so the angle can move when heated. An allowance of ¼ inch (6 mm) at each end of the steel lintel shall be provided for expansion. Steel angles should never be mortared tightly.

The lintel may also be reinforced masonry. Reinforced masonry lintels require no expansion provisions.

2.10   Smoke Chamber

The smoke chamber is located directly above the firebox and may be constructed of solid masonry.

Immediately behind the damper is the smoke shelf which is necessary to check downdrafts. Any downdrafts strike the smoke shelf and are diverted upward by the damper assembly.   The smoke shelf may be curved to assist in this process, but flat smoke shelves perform adequately.

As shown in Figure 2-25, the smoke chamber should be constructed so that the side walls and front wall taper inward to form the support of the fireplace chimney. The chimney is to be centered on the width of the fireplace and the back of the flue liner is in alignment with the vertical surface of the smoke chamber. This configuration funnels the smoke and gases from the fire into the chimney.

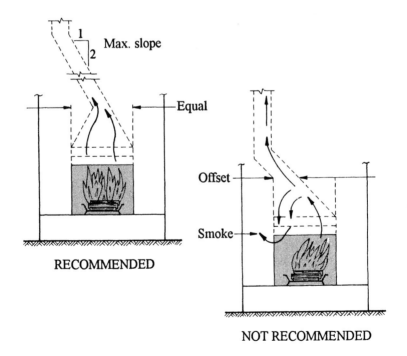

Figure 2-25   Smoke chamber must be equal on both sides in order to be efficient

2.11   Fireplace Construction

The fireplace hearth and side walls are constructed of a minimum of two inches (51 mm) of fire backs and six inches (152 mm) of mortar and masonry. Some building codes require that the firebox be constructed at a four inch (102 mm) minimum thickness, which means that the fire brick must be laid in the stretcher position. Note the firebox is surrounded by four inch (102 mm) solid brick for structural stability and thermal heat storage. Fire brick will not expand or contract significantly with the operating temperatures of residential fireplaces and chimneys.

There are two types of fireplace construction. One is constructed on concrete slab floors and the other is constructed in a frame floor using a cantilevered hearth.

A fireplace is constructed as follows: The fireplace is laid out, the back of the fireplace is constructed to a scaffold height of approximately five feet (1.5 m), and then the firebox is built and backfilled with tempered mortar. The area behind the firebox wall should not be grouted solidly but slushed loosely to allow for expansion of the firebox.

In earthquake zones 3 and 4, horizontal and vertical steel is required. The horizontal steel may be placed either in the mortar bed joint or in the grouted area.

Some fireboxes are constructed without the face, leaving ties so the face may be added at a later date, while other fireboxes are constructed simultaneously with the face. Either way is a satisfactory method of construction.

2.12   *Prefabricated Metal Air Circulating Fireboxes.*

A prefabricated metal air circulating firebox (Figures 2-26, 2-27 and 2-28) is built on the principles of a hot air furnace but retains all of the charm and glow of an open hearth fireplace. Any fuel may be used. The air chamber surrounding the firebox and upper throat draws in air, heats it and circulates it out through the outlet vents to help heat the home.   The firebox throat, damper and smoke chamber are all carefully engineered and factory-built for perfect operation.

Cool air is drawn through inlets at floor level and passes into the heating chambers where it is heated by contact with the hot metal. It is then returned and circulated to all parts of the immediate room and even into adjoining rooms. The circulation of warm air is the key principle in how a metal firebox improves the energy efficiency of the masonry fireplace.

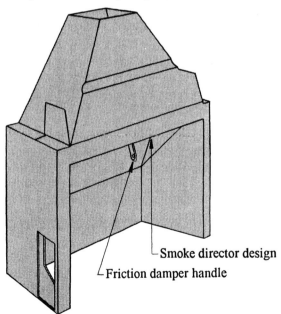

Smoke director design

Friction damper handle

Figure 2-26   Front view of prefabricated metal air circulating firebox

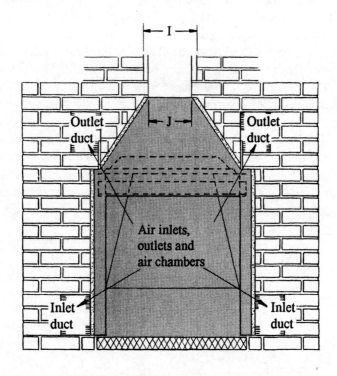

ELEVATION

Figure 2-27 Elevation of prefabricated metal air circulating fireplace

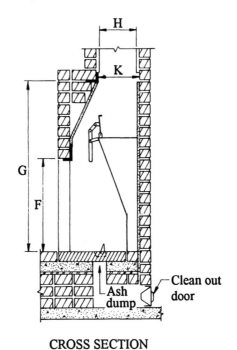

CROSS SECTION

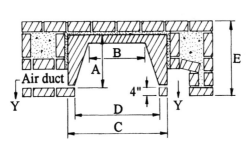

PLAN

See Table 2-D for dimensions.

Figure 2-28   Cross-section and plan of prefabricated metal air circulating fireplace

43

Table 2-D — Prefab Fireplace Specifications -- Standard Dimensions

Unit Depth A	Log length B	Unit width C	Finished opening width D	Minimum masonry depth E	Finished opening height F
inches (mm)	inches (mm)	inches (mm)	inches (mm)	inches (mm)	inches (mm)
19 ¾ (502)	23 (584)	39 ¾ (1010)	32 (813)	28 ¾ (730)	27 (686)
19 ¾ (502)	26 (660)	42¾ (1086)	35 (889)	28 ¾ (730)	27 (686)
19 ¾ (502)	31 (787)	47 ¾ (1213)	40 (1016)	28 ¾ (730)	27 (686)
24 ½ (622)	36 ½ (927)	52 ½ (1334)	47 (1194)	33 ¼ (857)	31 (787)

Table 2-D — Prefab Fireplace Specifications -- Standard Dimensions (Continued)

Unit Depth A	Height to top of dome G	Flue depth * H	Flue width * I	Unit opening J	Unit opening K
inches (mm)	inches (mm)	inches (mm)	inches (mm)	inches (mm)	inches (mm)
19 ¾ (502)	48½ (1232)	12 (305)	16 (406)	12 (305)	12 (305)
19 ¾ (502)	50¾ (1289)	12 (305)	16 (406)	12 (305)	12 (305)
19 ¾ (502)	54½ (1384)	16 (406)	16 (406)	12 (305)	12 (305)
24 ½ (622)	54½ (1384)	16 (406)	20 (508)	20 (508)	16 (406)

*Modular flue size for chimney less than 20 inches (508 mm) high shown

2.13   Ash Dumps and Cleanouts

Ash dumps are openings in the floor of the inner hearth where accumulated ashes can be shoveled. The ash pit below the firebox provides a non-combustible chamber that can be filled with ashes from over a long period of time and then emptied periodically.

Cleanout openings may be in the rear or side of the ash pit compartment and of sufficient area and volume below the floor of the firebox to allow easy access and removal of accumulated ashes.

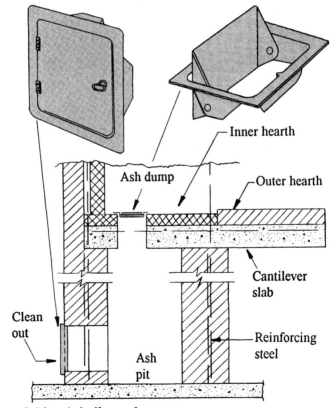

Figure 2-29   Ash disposal system

2.14   Gas Log Lighter

The gas shutoff valve should be an approved A.G.A. component and must be located outside the masonry fireplace and not embedded in the outside hearth. A swing joint, consisting of at least three elbows, should be installed between the gas shutoff valve and the log lighter pipe. This is to prevent breaks in the joints in the event of movement or settlement of the fireplace.

It is recommended that the gas log lighter be one inch (25 mm) above the ash bed and not buried in the ashes or in sand.

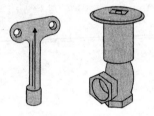

Figure 2-30   Gas shut-off valve

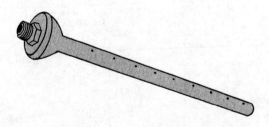

Figure 2-31   Log lighter of cast iron with air shutter and ½ inch (13 mm) pipe connection for gas line

Continuous burning pilot lights are not allowed. Indoor air vented to the outside to cool a firebox jacket is also prohibited.

EXCEPTION: When a gas log, log lighter or decorative gas appliance is installed in a fireplace, the flue damper shall be blocked open if required by the manufacturer's installation instructions or the California State Mechanical Code.

2.15   Clearances

2.15.1   Masonry Clearances

Wood or other combustible material shall be at least six inches (152 mm) away from the fireplace opening.   All combustible material shall be kept away from the chimney through a concealed space, a minimum distance two inches (51 mm) in accordance with applicable code.

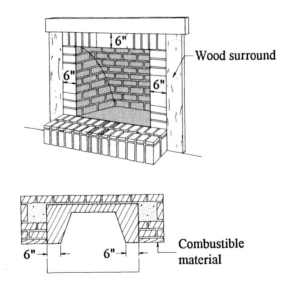

Figure 2-32   Clearances of combustible from fireplace opening and chimney

All combustible material shall be kept away from the chimney a minimum distance of two inches (51 mm) in accordance with applicable code.

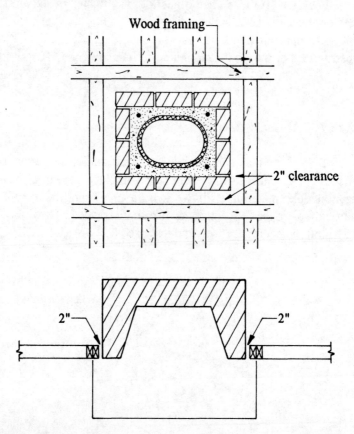

Figure 2-33 Clearances of combustible materials from chimney

2.15.2 *Metal Chimney Clearances*

Metal chimneys may be installed in a wood framed structure which may be covered with stucco, thin brick, wood shakes or other material.

The National Fire Protection Association, (NFPA) publication NFPA 211 Chimneys, Fireplaces, Vents and Solid Burning Appliances, 1992 Edition, provides guidelines for proper clearances.

The NFPA defines clearance as "The distance between a heat-producing appliance, chimney, chimney connector, vents, vent connector or plenum and other surfaces "

The following are excerpts from NFPA 211.

4-1.5   Metal chimneys shall have sufficient clearance from buildings and structures to avoid heating combustible material to a temperature in excess of 90°F (50°C) above ambient and to permit inspection and maintenance operations on the chimney.   They shall be located or shielded to avoid danger or burns to persons.

4-1.7   Metal chimney serving residential-type or low-heat appliances and producing flue gases having a temperature below 350°F (165.5°C) at the entrance to the chimney at full load or partial load shall be lined with acid and condensate resistant metal or refractory material, constructed of suitable stainless steel, or otherwise protected to minimize or prevent condensation and corrosion damage.

4-2   Metal Chimneys for Residential-type or Low-Heat Appliances.

4-2.2   Clearances

4-2.2.1   Exterior

4-2.2.1.1 Exterior metal chimneys used only for residential-type or low-heat appliances as defined in Table 1-2(a) shall have a clearance of not less than 18 in. (457 mm) from a wall of wood frame construction and from any combustible material.

4-2.2.1 2 Exterior metal chimneys over 18 in. (457 mm) in diameter shall have a clearance of not less than 4 in. (102 mm) from a building wall of other than wood frame construction.

4-2.2.1.3 Exterior metal chimneys 18 in. (457 mm) or less in diameter shall have a clearance of not less than 2 in. (51 mm) from a building wall of other than wood frame construction.

4-2.2.2   Interior

4-2.2.2.1 Where a metal chimney extends through any story of a building above that in which the appliances connected to the chimney are installed, it shall be enclosed in such upper stories, within a continuous enclosure constructed of noncombustible materials (*see Section 1-5*). The enclosure shall comply with the following:

(a)   The enclosure shall so extend from the ceiling of the appliance room to or through the roof as to maintain the integrity of the fire separations required by the applicable building code provisions.

(b)   The enclosure walls shall have a fire resistance rating of not less than 1 hr. if the building is less than 4 stories in height.

(c)   The enclosure walls shall have a fire resistance rating of not less than 2 hr. if the building is 4 stories or more in height.

(d)   The enclosure shall provide a space on all sides of the chimney sufficient to permit inspection and repair, but in no case shall it be less than 12 in. (305 mm).

(e)   The enclosing wall shall be without openings.

Exception: Doorways equipped with approved self-closing fire doors shall be permitted to be installed at various floor levels for inspection purposes.

4-2 2.2.2   Where a metal chimney serving only residential-type or low-heat appliances as defined in Table 1-2(a) is located in the same story of a building as that in which the appliances connected thereto are located, it shall have a clearance of not less than 18 in. (457 mm) from a wall of wood frame construction and from any combustible material.

4-2.2.2.3   Interior metal chimneys over 18 in. (457 mm) in diameter shall have a clearance of not less then 4 in. (102 mm) from a building wall of other than wood frame construction.

4-2.2.2.4   Interior metal chimneys 18 in (457 mm) or less in diameter shall have a clearance of not less than 2 in. (51 mm) from a building wall of other than wood frame construction.

4-2 2.2.5   Where a metal chimney serving only residential-type or low-heat appliances as defined in Table 1-2(a) passes through a roof constructed of combustible material, it shall be guarded by a ventilating thimble of galvanized steel or approved corrosion-resistant metal, extending not less than 9 in. (229 mm) below and 9 in. (229 mm) above the roof construction and of a size to provide not less than 6 in. (152 mm) clearance on all sides of the chimney.

Exception: In lieu of the above requirement, the combustible material in the roof construction shall be permitted to be cut away to provide not less than 18 in. (457 mm) clearance on all sides of the chimney, with any material used to close up such opening entirely noncombustible.

Reprinted with permission from NFPA 211, Sections 4-1.5, 4-1.7 and 4-2.2, Copyright © 1992, National Fire Protection Association, Quincy, MA 02269. This reprinted material is not complete. The official position of the National Fire Protection Association on the subject is represented only by the standard in its entirety.

Figure 2-34   Mantel

2.16   Mantels

Wood mantels should be detailed to provide proper clearances from fireplace openings. Mantels may project $\frac{1}{8}$ inch (3 mm) for each one inch (25 mm) away or above the opening. Therefore a mantel ten inch (254 mm) above the opening may only project $\frac{1}{8}$ inch x 10 inches (3 mm x 254 mm) = 1¼ inches (32 mm).

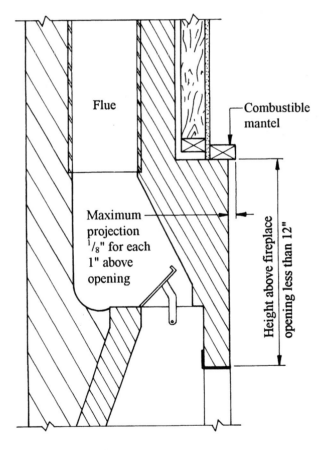

Figure 2-35   Projection of combustible mantel less than 12 inches (305 mm) above the fireplace opening

However, there is no projection limitation for mantels twelve inches (305 mm) or more above the opening.

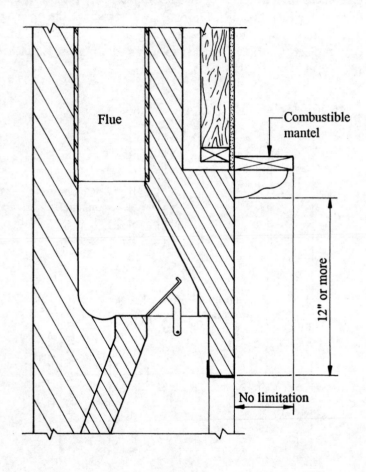

Figure 2-36 Projection of combustible mantel 12 inches (305 mm) or greater above fireplace opening

DAMPERS

3.1 General

A good damper is one of the most important items installed in a well-designed fireplace. It forms the throat passage through which gases and smoke pass from the fire chamber to the smoke chamber. Correctly placed, it assists in directing heat into the room while affording exit for smoke.

For efficient operation the damper should be closed when the fireplace is not in use. When starting a fire, open the damper fully and reduce the opening size once the fire starts to maximize the heat. Be careful not to close the damper too much or smoke will travel back into the room.

The damper's movable part, the valve plate, governs the volume of discharge and can be adjusted to close the flue opening completely when desired and thus avoid drafts in the room when the fireplace is not in use. When closed, it prevents rodents and insects from entering the home and prevents loss of furnace heat in winter and cool air in summer.

There are several types of dampers, such as blade damper (Figure 3-3), form damper (Figure 3-4), high dome or high form damper (Figures 3-7, 3-8 and 3-10), the universal or square form damper (Figure 3-12) and the chimney top damper (Figure 3-13).

The last two types of dampers may be used on multi-opening fireplaces

Some dampers operate by means of a push-and-pull-handle, some with a poker, others with a twist handle, rotary turn screw control or opening-and-closing chains Rotary control mechanisms have gained popularity as users don't have to reach into the hot firebox to adjust the damper, thereby eliminating the chance of being burned Dampers should be set loosely in place to allow for expansion

Dampers are a requirement and must be used in all fireplaces. They are located in the forward part of the fireplace to allow for a smoke shelf They should be no less than six inches to eight inches (152 mm to 203 mm) above the top of the fireplace opening

From the 1994 UBC Sec 3102 7 9

Metal dampers equivalent to not less than 0.097 inch (2.46 mm) (No. 12 carbon sheet metal gage) steel shall be installed. When fully opened, damper openings shall not be less than 90 percent of the required flue area

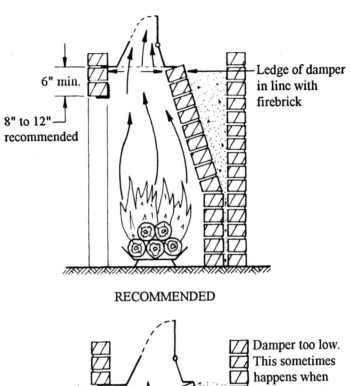

6" min.

8" to 12"—
recommended

Ledge of damper
in line with
firebrick

RECOMMENDED

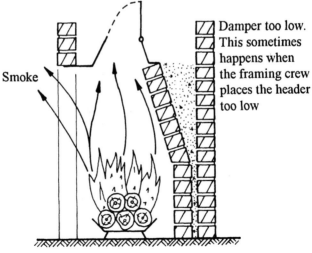

Smoke

Damper too low.
This sometimes
happens when
the framing crew
places the header
too low

NOT RECOMMENDED

Figure 3-1   A right and wrong installation of blade dampers

The damper must be the full width of the firebox. Corbeling the firebox to fit a smaller damper is not permitted

When fully opened, dampers should stand vertically at least ½ inch (13 mm) to the room side of the vertical projection of the inner face of the flue (Figure 3-7). This is to prevent rain and downdraft from entering the firebox. This offset also acts as a buffer to return downdraft wind currents back up the chimney flue, thus assuring good draft and a smoke-free operation.

When fully opened, damper openings should not be less than 90% of the required flue area.

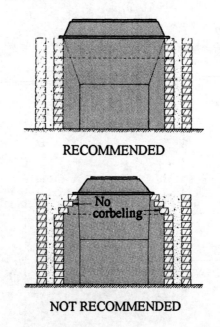

RECOMMENDED

NOT RECOMMENDED

Figure 3-2   Correct size and width of damper is necessary for proper functioning of fireplace

See manufacturer's catalogues for details of dimensions, available sizes and installation instructions.

3.2   Blade Damper

One of the earliest forms of dampers is the blade damper, which is heavy gauge sheet metal with rolled edges for stiffness with a handle welded to the plate for opening and closing the flue.   The smoke chamber is carefully formed above it and requires skill in its proper construction.

The oldest type of damper is the cast-iron blade damper.   Its sturdy cast-iron construction resists warping and burning out.

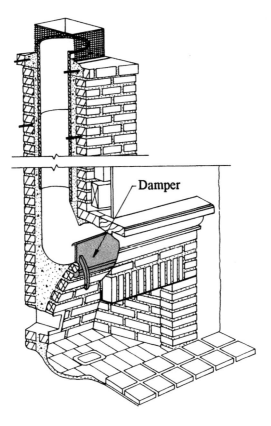

Figure 3-3   Blade damper

3.3 *Form Damper*

The form damper (Figures 3-4, 3-5 and 3-6) is more elaborate than the simple blade damper for it incorporates the control damper blade with a metal form to simplify and reduce labor costs in constructing the throat between the firebox and the flue. On some form dampers a mineral wool blanket covers the metal form, which will allow for expansion of the metal.

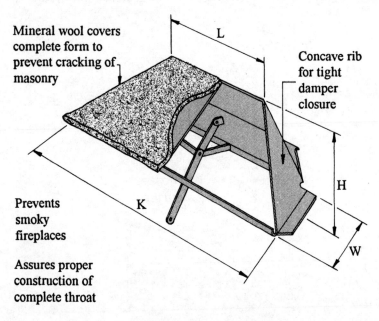

Mineral wool covers complete form to prevent cracking of masonry

Concave rib for tight damper closure

L

H

W

K

Prevents smoky fireplaces

Assures proper construction of complete throat

See Table 3-A for dimensions

Figure 3-4   Form damper

The form damper is for single opening fireplaces only as its throat capacity may be insufficient for multiple openings.

When installing a form damper, it is important to cover the complete form with mineral wool and use double thickness at each end.

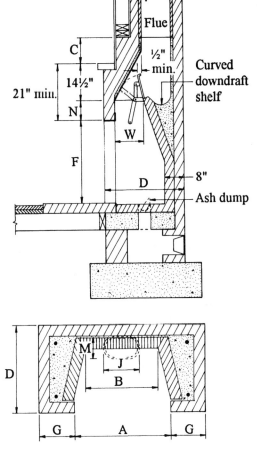

See Table 3-A for dimensions

Figure 3-5   Cross-section thru single face fireplace using a form damper

Table 3-A — Key to Figures 3-4 and 3-5

A	B	C Min.	D	F	G	H Min.
In.	In.	In.	In.	In.	In.	In.
24-26	17	6	27+	24-27	13+	14½
27-32	23	6	27+	24-27	13+	14½
33-38	27	6	31+	27-30	13+	14½
39-43	33	9	31+	30-33	13+	14½
44-51	39	12	31+	33-36	16½ +	16½
52-57	43	12	42+	36-42	16½ +	16½
58-64	49	15	42+	36-42	16½ +	16½
65-74	61	18	42+	36-48	16½ +	16½

Table 3-A — Key to Figures 3-4 and 3-5 (Continued)

A	J	K	L	M	N Min.	W
In.	In.	In.	In.	In.	In.	In.
24-26	13	24	8½	9	6	10
27-32	13	29	13½	9	6	10
33-38	13	35	19½	13	6	10
39-43	17	41	25½	13	6	10
44-51	21	47	31½	13	9	10
52-57	21	54	44½	21	9	13
58-64	21	60	50½	21	9	13
65-74	25	72	62½	21	9	13

NOTE   For dimensions in mm, multiply inches by 25 4
               For area in sq mm multiply sq in by 645 2

Construction of masonry fireplace showing installation of damper

3.4   High-Form or High-Dome Damper

The high-dome or high-form damper (Figures 3-6, 3-7, 3-8 3-9, and 3-10) can be used for multiple opening fireplaces and has a built-in downdraft shelf, which permits the chimney flue to be located directly above the firebox.   This saves 20-25% of material and labor that would be necessary to offset the chimney flue as required in other designs in order to provide a separate downdraft shelf and to prevent smoke trouble.

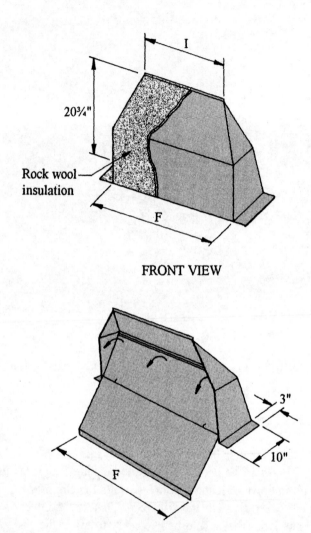

FRONT VIEW

REAR VIEW

Figure 3-6   High-form or high-dome damper

The high-form damper is used with fireplaces that have openings on front and sides or a through fireplace with opening on front and back.

This specially designed, modern high-dome or high-form damper is built to promote maximum draft efficiency and permit a deeper downdraft shelf design without special attention to throat construction. Extra height and width are built in, allowing shallower fireplace construction (consuming less floor space), yct still giving the ultimate in operational satisfaction. With no need to form a throat of brick, stone or mortar, construction costs and labor are consequently reduced.

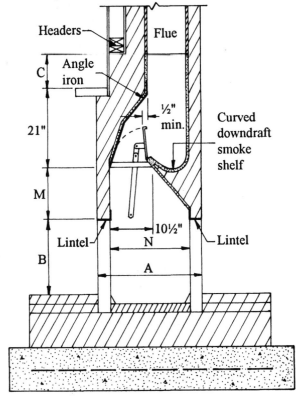

Section for plan #2 and plan #3

See Table 3-B for Dimensions

Figure 3-7   Cross-section of multi-face fire place using high-dome dampers

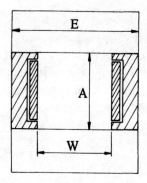
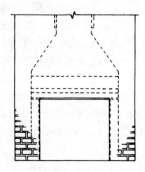

PLAN 2
OPEN THROUGH

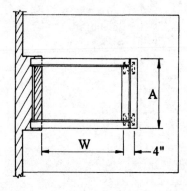
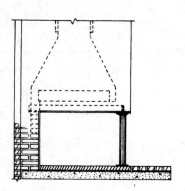

PLAN 3
3 WAY OPENING

See Table 3-B for dimensions

Figure 3-8   Plan cross-section multi-face fireplaces using high-dome dampers

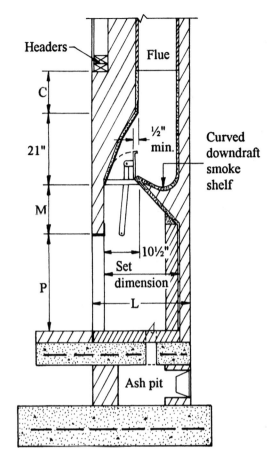

Section for plan #1 and plan #4

See Table 3-B for dimensions

Figure 3-9   Cross-section of multi-face fireplace using high-dome dampers

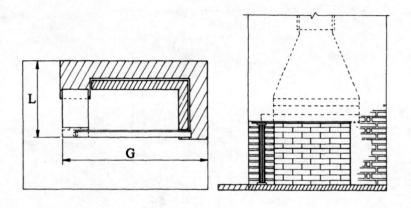

PLAN 1
DOUBLE OPENING

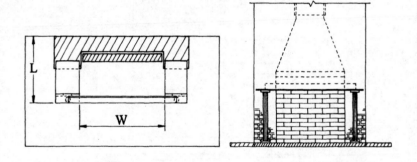

PLAN 4
3 WAY OPENING

See Table 3-B for dimensions

Figure 3-10   Plan cross-section of multi-face fireplaces using high-dome dampers

Table 3-B — Key to Figures 3-6, 3-7, 3-8, 3-9 and 3-10
Dimensions in Inches and Millimeters

A Min.	B	C	E	F	G	I
In. (mm)	In. (mm)	In. (mm)	In. (mm)	In. (mm)	In. (mm)	In. (mm)
30 (762)	21 (533)	6 (152)	45½ (1156)	28 (711)	41¼ (1048)	19 (483)
30 (762)	21 (533)	9 (229)	51½ (1308)	34 (864)	47¼ (1200)	25 (635)
30 (762)	21 (533)	12 (305)	57½ (1461)	40 (1016)	53¼ (1353)	31 (787)
34¼ (883)	21 (533)	15 (381)	64½ (1638)	46 (1168)	59¼ (1505)	37 (940)

Table 3-B — Key to Figures 3-6, 3-7, 3-8, 3-9 and 3-10
(Continued Dimensions in Inches and Millimeters)

A Min.	L	M	N	P	W	O.D. Flue
In. (mm)	In. (mm)	In. (mm)	In. (mm)	In. (mm)	In. (mm)	In. (mm)
30 (762)	30 (762)	15 (381)	23 (584)	27 (686)	29 (737)	13x17 (330x432)
30 (762)	30 (762)	15 (381)	23 (584)	27 (686)	35 (898)	13x21 (330x533)
30 (762)	30 (762)	15 (381)	23 (584)	27 (686)	41 (1041)	13x21 (330x533)
34¼ (883)	34¼ (883)	18 (457)	27 (686)	30 (762)	47 (1194)	17x21 (432x533)

3.5   *Universal or Square Form Damper*

The universal or square form damper (Figure 3-11) is applicable to all types of fireplaces. Fireplaces with more than one side need a damper shaped to help promote the even burning of the fire everywhere on the hearth. A high funnel shape and larger throat area help to solve this problem.

This integral unit, containing damper, smoke chamber and lintel, is the practical answer to multi-opening fireplace construction. The deep, smooth-sloping sides of the dome assure good draft while permitting unobstructed "see through" design.

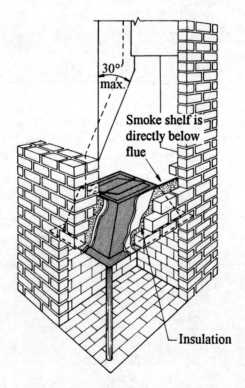

Figure 3-11   Universal or square form damper

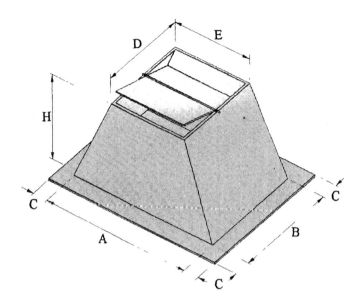

See Table 3-C for Dimensions

Figure 3-12   Installation example of a universal or square form damper

Table 3-C — Key to Figure 3-12

Overall Size A x B	Flue Outlet D x E	Overall Height H	Lintel Size C
Inches (mm)	Inches (mm)	Inches (mm)	Inches (mm)
3 x 22 (864 x 559)	19 x 18 (483 x 457)	16 (406)	3½ (89)
40 x 22 (1016 x 559)	19 x 24 (483 x 610)	16 (406)	3½ (89)
47 x 22 (1194 x 559)	19 x 30 (483 x 702)	16 (406)	3½ (890)

3.6   *Chimney Top Damper*

The chimney top damper, as shown in Figure 3-13, permits the chimney and flue to be heated and maintain heat for improved draft. It must be weight or spring loaded so as to be in an open position if the controlling mechanism fails. This is necessary so that the chimney will not close during a fire and cause a smoking and dangerous fireplace

Chimney top dampers can be used with any type of fireplace, and since they protect the fireplace from the top, chimney top dampers also function as chimney caps when closed. If the internal throat damper becomes non-functional, a chimney top damper can be readily installed to keep the fireplace functional.

Chimney top dampers work efficiently for fireplaces that are used as a primary heat source when the damper is closed after the fire is out. They are also appropriate for Rumford fireplaces as most internal dampers don't fit them due to the small Rumford throat.

There is one drawback to chimney top dampers. Being exposed to the elements, the moving parts may freeze when the temperature drops, making this type of damper inoperable.

Selection of the proper damper size is important to insure good flow of air and improved suction to increase the draft of smoke and products of combustion from the firebox.

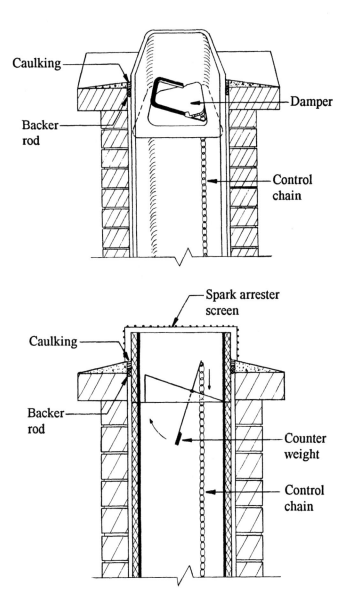

Caulking

Damper

Backer rod

Control chain

Spark arrester screen

Caulking

Backer rod

Counter weight

Control chain

Figure 3-13   Chimney top damper

3.7   *Exhaust Fan on Top of Chimney*

Good draft in a fireplace insures maximum combustion of the fuel and improves fuel economy.

Many times it is necessary to improve the draft or draw.

This may be due to a too large fireplace opening and too small a flue or could be from other causes.

Downdrafts from prevailing winds and hilly terrain may cause faulty drafts in the chimney.

To improve the draft in a fireplace, a chimney fan installed on the top of the chimney forces air through the fireplace and up the chimney.

This exhaust fan draws the products of combustion (e.g. smoke) up the flue and prevents them from pouring into the room.

It ensures a perfect draft despite unfavorable conditions in the fireplace or chimney.

It also corrects faults due to the location of a house in relation to prevailing winds.

An exhaust fan can be fitted on the top of the flue, bolted and anchored to the chimney and by means of a variable rheostat, voltage regulator can adjust the magnitude of the draft.

A correctly installed exhaust chimney fan will solve a number of fireplace problems:

1. **Badly proportioned chimney**
    The up draft on the chimney may be severely restricted if the flue is too small or if there are too many bends in the chimney.

2. **Chimney is too short**
    Even though a chimney meets the Building Codes, it may be too short to allow flue gases to escape, due to insufficient draft.

3. **Chimney to external wall**
    If one or more sides of the chimney is part of an external wall, this could cause cooling of the chimney, reducing draft.

4. **Back drafts**
    A perfectly designed chimney cannot always guarantee back drafts not to occur. Tall trees or buildings around the chimney have influence on wind direction and can cause back draft.

5. **Badly designed fireplace**
    The fireplace itself can release smoke into the room if its proportions are wrong.

6. **Insulation**
    When houses are efficiently insulated, there is a risk that the hearth cannot draw sufficient air for combustion, thereby causing smoke in the room.

7. **Ventilation**
    Ventilation in a room or a ventilation fan may produce pressure changes so that the smoke is pulled into the room and not up the chimney.

Information courtesy of Sleepy Hollow Chimney Supply, Ltd., suppliers of EXHAUSTO Chimney Fan, 85 Emjay Blvd., Brentwood, NY 11717.

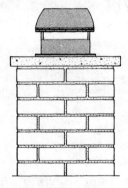

ELEVATION VIEW

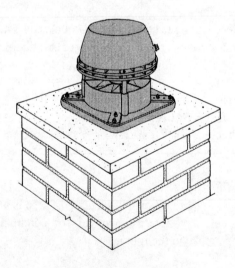

AXONOMETRIC VIEW

Figure 3-14   The Exhausto Chimney Fan is a simple way to improve the draft in the chimney

SECTION 4

ENERGY CONSERVATION

4.1   Energy Efficiency with Fireplaces

4.1.1   Outside Air Inlet

One way to increase the efficiency of a fireplace is to use air from outside the structure for combustion and draft. Conventional fireplaces draw air from the room that has already been heated; the drop in room air pressure caused by this air loss can result in increased infiltration.

There are many ways in which outside air can be brought into the firebox area. One example is shown in Figures 4-1, 4-2 and 4-3. In general, whatever method is chosen will require three basic parts, which are the **intake,** the **passageway** and the **inlet.** To keep the fireplace from becoming a source of infiltration when not in use, tight fitting inlet dampers that are readily closable are recommended.

Intake: The intake should be located on an outside wall or in the back of the fireplace. A screen-backed louver is required. Codes do not permit the intake to be located within the garage. Other possible locations for the intake are in a crawl space or other unheated areas.

Passageway: A noncombustible passageway or duct connects the intake to the inlet. Many options are available as to the size and material used for the passageway. Ducts ranging from approximately six square inches (0.003 m²) to 55 square inches (0.035 m²) have been used successfully. The size of the duct should be in relation to the size of the fireplace. The passageway can be built into the base of the fireplace assembly or channeled between floor joists.

It can also enter above the base of the fireplace and connect to inlets located in the sides of the firebox.

Inlet: The inlet brings the outside air into the firebox. A damper is required to control the volume and direction of the air. This is necessary because cold exterior air brought into the fireplace expands when heated and could result in more air than is needed for combustion and thus create roll-off smoke into the room.

The inlet can be located in the sides or the floor of the combustion chamber, preferably in front of the grate. If the inlet is located toward the back of the combustion chamber, ashes may be blown into the room, either by downdrafts from the flue or updrafts through the inlet.

A potential problem due to increased velocity of the air coming through the inlet is that the temperature within the combustion chamber can be increased significantly. This can result in grates and inlet dampers being literally burned up as a result of higher temperatures. To help decrease the velocity of the air through the inlet, a space before the inlet should be constructed as a stilling chamber, as shown in Figure 4-1.

For example the California Code requires only six square inches (0.003 m²) of external air intake port, but this may be too small for good combustion when the glass doors are closed. Glass doors may inhibit efficient combustion by upsetting a good air to fuel ratio, although with sufficient external air this may not happen. If doors are to be closed during combustion and during the following period of heat radiation, then they should be made of a material transparent to the energy wavelengths used to transmit the heat to the dwelling.

A minimum of one 16 sq. in. (0.010 m^2) air inlet port should be installed, and if this is insufficient to prevent the fire from smoking and sputtering, use two 16 sq. in. (0.010 m^2) inlet ports either on the back wall or one on each side wall.

Exterior air vents are not required, although may be beneficial, if the fireplace is located on a slab on grade away from the exterior wall.

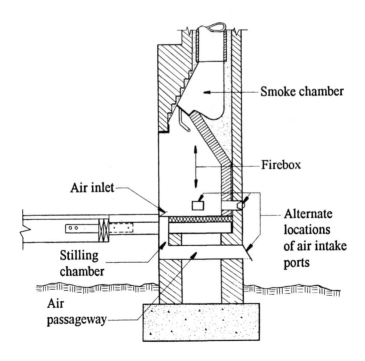

Figure 4-1   Single-face fireplace cross section showing outside air intakes

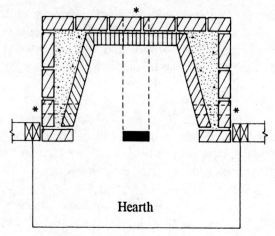

*Alternate locations
of outside air inlet vents

Figure 4-2   Single-face fireplace plan with alternate outside air vents

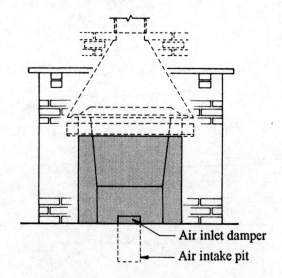

Air inlet damper

Air intake pit

Figure 4-3   Single-face fireplace front elevation with alternate outside air vents

4.1.2   Glass Fireplace Screens

A glass screen should be used on both conventional fireplaces and fireplaces with an outside air supply. These screens should be closed when the fire is out, when the fire is smoldering and before it is safe to close the damper because of flue gases and smoke. Glass screens provide a barrier that keeps heated air from escaping up the chimney but still allows residual smoke and fumes to escape.

These screens should be sealed around the edges and have tight-fitting doors and vents so that the fireplace is not a source of infiltration when not in use. It may be that the radiated energy stopped by the glass screen may be greater than the convected energy contained in the room air.

Caution is necessary when fireplaces are operated with the glass screens in a closed position. Increased temperatures due to higher air velocity through intakes may cause problems, such as the fire being blown out or the glass doors shattering.

Glass fireplace screen

4.1.3 Installation of Fireplaces, Decorative Gas Appliances and Gas Logs [§150(e)]

Excerpt from California Energy Commission Requirements 1992, Chapter 2, Section 2.2.

Because conditioned air can escape through a fireplace chimney, fireplace efficiency can be greatly improved through proper air control which the Standards require in the form of specific air control measures.

Installation of masonry fireplaces shall include:

• Closable metal or glass doors covering the entire opening of the firebox which can be closed when the fire is burning.

• A combustion air intake to draw air from the outside of the building directly into the firebox. This intake must be at least six square inches (3,871 sq. mm) in area and be equipped with a readily accessible, operable and tight-fitting damper.

   Outside combustion air intakes are not required in the Standards if the fireplace is installed over a concrete slab and will not be located on an exterior wall.

• A flue damper with a readily accessible control.

   These requirements do not apply to free-standing stoves.

   Continuous burning pilot lights are not allowed. Indoor air vented to the outside to cool a firebox jacket is also prohibited.

NOTE: When a gas log, log lighter, or decorative gas appliance is installed in a fireplace, the flue damper shall be blocked open if required by the manufacturer's installation instructions or the State Mechanical Code.

4.1.4   Wood Heating

NOTE: Excerpt from California Energy Commission Requirement, 1992, Chapter 2, Section 8.6

4.1.4.1   Wood Space Heating

Only "wood heaters" as established by the Federal Environmental Protection Agency (Federal Register, Vol. 52, No. 32, February 18, 1987) can be used to show compliance with the Standards. If not for compliance with the Standards, wood heaters need only meet safety requirements. Check with the local building department for these conditions.

The Environmental Protection Agency (EPA) defines a wood heater as:

.... an enclosed, wood burning appliance used for space heating, domestic water heating, or indoor cooking that meets all of the following criteria:

1.   An air-to-fuel ratio averaging less than 35-to-1.
2.   Firebox volume less than 20 cubic feet (0.6 cubic meter).
3.   Minimum burn rate less than 5 kilogram/hour (11.0 lbs/hr), and
4.   Maximum weight of less than 800 kilogram (1762 lbs).

The federal rules explicitly exclude furnaces, boilers and open fireplaces, but include wood heater inserts.

4.2   Masonry Fireplace Construction with Consideration to Pollution Emissions and Efficiency of Heating

The design of masonry fireplaces to minimize air polluting emissions and maximize energy is in a transition stage. The goal is to achieve maximum heat output from a residential fireplace while minimizing smoke. Considerations that help minimize polluting emissions while maximizing fuel efficiency are:

1.   Use dry fuel.

2.   Provide sufficient air for combustion.

In the 1790's Count Rumford brought masonry fireplace design into the modern age by using small logs in a small fireplace to produce more heat. He accomplished this by changing the throat design to keep the air flowing efficiently. Rumford also changed the shape of the firebox to radiate this increased heat output into the room (see page 13).

When designing a masonry fireplace it is important to understand that toxic emissions are the by-products of incompletely burned fuel. Complete combustion results in higher heat output and reduced toxic emissions. In other words, the air pollution from a fireplace is unused fuel. The pollution is greatest during the kindling stage, as such, the use of natural gas to start kindling significantly cuts pollution.

Design considerations that aid in increasing heat output and/or reducing toxic emissions include the following:

1.   Maximize chimney height to increase draw. This increases negative pressure above the fire, resulting in more combustion air being drawn into the active combustion zone.

2.   Round the transition from the horizontal bottom of the lintel to the vertical forward wall of the smoke chamber to minimize any turbulence (see pages 18 and 20).

3.   Design the angle of the covings in the fireplace to radiate the heat into the room (see page 19).

4.   Use as much masonry as practical to provide a large heat sink.

5.   Locate the fireplace inside the room. If it must be on an outside wall, then have the fireplace flush with the exterior wall, not protruding from the exterior wall and insulate the masonry from the exterior exposure.

6.   Provide natural gas log lighters.

7.   Design the fireplace to use preformed smoke chambers, throat and flue tile to minimize friction on the byproducts of combustion and dilution air.

8.   Locate the flue directly over the firebox for the direct flow of smoke.

Regulations addressing masonry fireplace emissions are in the early stages of development.   Most regulations refer to permissible emission levels as grams of pollution per hour or rate of pollution emissions. More recent emission regulations express permissible emission levels as grams of pollution per kilogram of fuel, a factor of pollution emissions. When designing a fireplace to minimize pollution per kilogram of fuel, a large fireplace provides the lowest emission levels, as a large fire tends to burn fuel more completely. When designing a fireplace to minimize pollution per hour of time, a small fireplace will provide the lowest emission levels, as small fire generates less emissions per hour than a large fire.

The future of emission regulations appears to be heading for maximum limitations based on grams of pollution per kilogram of fuel. Properly designed wood burning masonry fireplaces are efficient sources of energy producing low total emissions as expressed in grams per kilograms of fuel.

The idea that masonry fireplaces create relatively more pollution than metal fireplaces or metal wood stoves is not correct. Very simply put, combustion is oxidation and oxidation is corrosion and corrosion leads to pollution.

A fireplace can be viewed as a large containment vessel for the oxidation or combustion of a fire. For complete oxidizing reactions (less pollution), we want oxidizing conditions. Oxidizing conditions present in a metal combustion chamber or containment vessel (metal fireplace or metal stove) will eventually compromise the walls of the chamber or vessel resulting in the release of igniting gases and/or solids or pollution.

Masonry fireplace with side air inlets

CHIMNEYS and FLUES

5.1 Chimney Requirements

The chimney consists of a flue liner and a chimney wall and is constructed directly on the smoke chamber. The chimney. The chimney wall shall be constructed so that there is at least a four inch (102 mm) nominal thickness of solid masonry between the flue liner and any exterior surfaces. Solid masonry products for chimney wall construction (brick, block or stone) are those that are either 100% solid or those with cores or holes of any configuration that do not exceed 25% of the cross-sectional area of any load bearing surface.

When a chimney contains more than one flue, adjacent flues must have a separation between them. The separation is to be constructed of solid masonry wythes (partitions) not less than four inches (102 mm), nominal, in thickness and the partitions shall be bonded to the chimney walls. One flue should be at least four inches (102 mm) higher than the adjacent flue.

The chimney must extend at least two feet (0.6 m) above the highest point where it passes through the roof. In addition, the top of the chimney should be at least two feet (0.6 m) above any portion of the building or surrounding buildings that may be within ten feet (3 m) of the chimney.

Good draft is normally achieved if chimney height is such that the vertical distance from the top of the fireplace throat to the top of the chimney is 15 feet (4.6 m). If the chimney is less than 15 feet (4.6 m), a larger flue size should be considered. Increased height can easily be obtained by the addition of a decorative chimney pot.

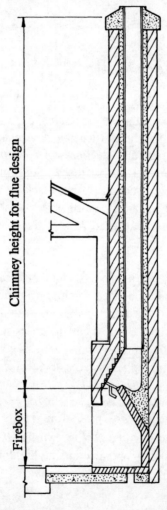

Figure 5-1   Height of chimney for determining size of flue

5.2   Flue Requirements

5.2.1   General

Fireplaces must have the correct flue area to function properly. The flue area is dependent on the size of the fireplace opening and the number of faces.

A flue that is too small will not provide an adequate draft. The fire will not burn well, and smoke will back up and pour out the front of the fireplace opening. Too large a flue can create too great a draft, causing the fire to burn vigorously; however, this may be regulated by closing down the damper.

Generally, the required flue area is approximately $^1/_{10}$ of the area of the fireplace opening; however, some codes may specify $^1/_8$ to $^1/_{12}$ under varying conditions. The flue area is determined by calculating the area of the fireplace opening and dividing by 10, thus obtaining the required effective cross-sectional area of the flue. The graphs (Figures 5-13 and 5-14) readily determine the flue size required for a single-face fireplace.

5.2.2   HUD and VA Requirements

HUD and VA require effective flue area to be $^1/_{10}$ the area of fireplace openings when the chimneys are 15 feet (4.6 m) high or more and $^1/_8$ of the fireplace opening when the chimney is less than 15 feet (4.6 m) high. The height of the chimney is measured from fireplace throat to top of chimney. When the height of the chimney is measured from the hearth to the top of the chimney, the ratio of flue area to fireplace opening area shall be $^1/_8$ for 15 feet (4.6 m) high or less; $^1/_{10}$ for 20 feet (6.1 m) high; and $^1/_{12}$ for 25 feet (7.6 m) high.

5.2.3   Single Face Fireplace

For a fireplace with a **single face** (Figure 5-2), the area of the fireplace opening is the height times the width.

Area = H x W

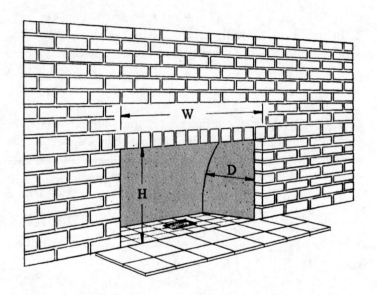

Figure 5-2   Single face fireplace

5.2.4   Two Faced Adjacent Fireplace

For a fireplace with **two faced adjacent** (Figure 5-3), the area of the fireplace opening to determine the size of the flue would be calculated as the diagonal distance between corners times the height of the fireplace.

$$\text{Area} = H\sqrt{D^2 + W^2}$$

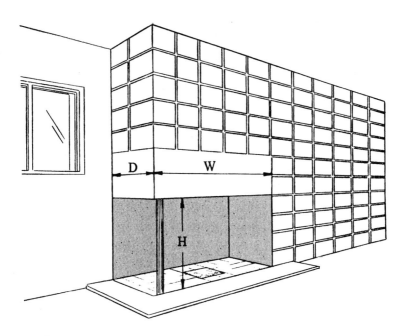

Figure 5-3   Two faced adjacent fireplace (L-shape)

91

5.2.5   Two Faced Opposite Fireplace

For a fireplace with **two faced opposite** (Figure 5-4), the area of the fireplace opening would be twice the width times the fireplace height.   **However, the FHA and VA do not recommend a fireplace that is open on two opposite sides,** generally called a see-through fireplace. **It is recommended that a fire screen of fire-resistant, tempered pyrex glass be placed on one side.** This glass will prevent the fire from blowing into the room and causing a fire hazard. When the two opposite face fireplace is sealed on one side with a tempered pyrex glass, the flue area of the fireplace opening is the height times the width of one opening.

Area = 2 (W x H) (without fire screen on one side
Area = (W x H) (with fire screen on one side)

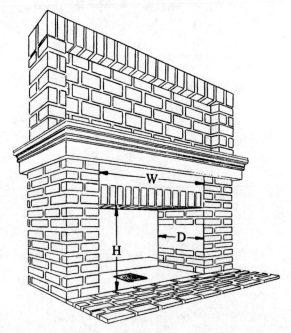

Figure 5-4   Two faced opposite fireplace (Look-thru)

5.2.6   Three Faced Fireplace (2 long, 1 short)

For a fireplace with **three faces which have two long and one short sides** (Figure 5-5), multiply twice the long side by the height to obtain the area of fireplace opening and to determine the required flue area.

Area = 2 (W x H)

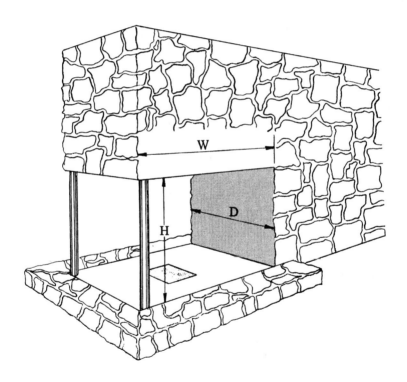

Figure 5-5   Three faced fireplace (2 long, 1 short)

5.2.7 Three Faced Fireplace (1 long, 2 short)

For a fireplace with **three faces which have one long and two short sides** (Figure 5-6), multiply the height of the fireplace by the sum of the long plus one short side to obtain the area of the fireplace opening in determining the required flue area.

Area = H (D + W)

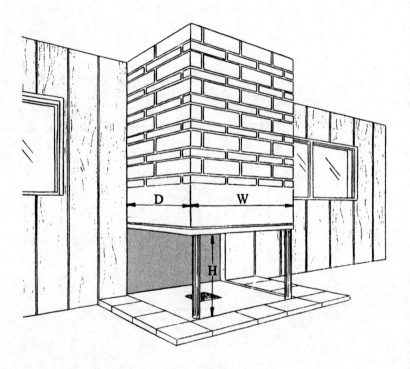

Figure 5-6   Three faced fireplace (1 long, 2 short)

5.2.8   Fire Pits

Fire pits (Figure 5-7) are very popular in family rooms, cocktail lounges, resort lobbies and similar places and are very pleasant to sit around. The area of the fireplace opening, which is used to determine the flue size, is computed as follows: 1.6 times the clear vertical height from the top of the fire ring to the bottom edge of the hood times the diameter of the hood. (See Figure 5-8).

Area = 1.6 (H x D)

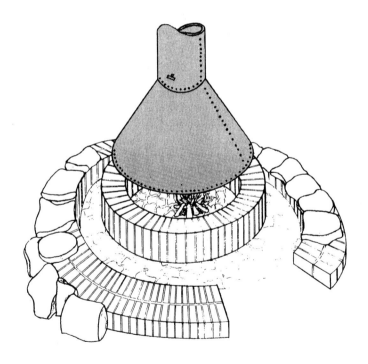

Figure 5-7   Fire pit with hood and flue

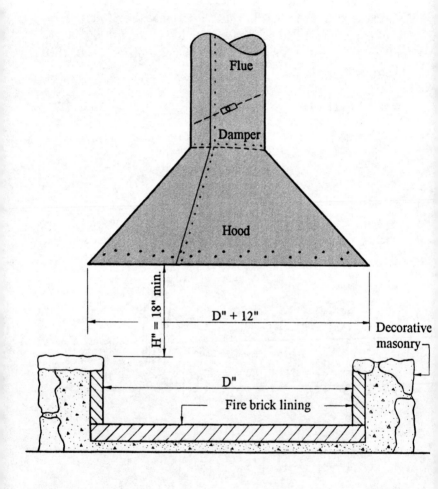

Figure 5-8   Cross-section of fire pit showing brick lining

5.3   Flue Sizes

The Chimney Design Committee of the American Society of Heating, Refrigerating and Air Conditioning Engineers (ASHRAE) recommends a round or radius-cornered flue be employed wherever practical, stating that such will provide a better draft than other shapes having equal cross-sectional areas and operating under the same conditions.

Radius corners prevent the problem of the dead corners of rectangular flues accumulating soot, which if not removed by periodic flue cleaning is likely to cause hazardous chimney fires. Also, the radius cornered design provides space between the flue lining and brickwork for steel reinforcing bars and grout to protect against damage from earthquake or ground settling.

Significant savings in time and materials result from the use of flue-lined chimney—the reinforced lined chimneys require only a single wythe of brick or block, whereas unlined chimneys require two wythes.

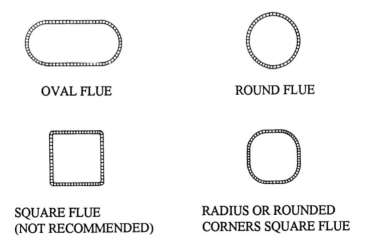

OVAL FLUE   ROUND FLUE

SQUARE FLUE   RADIUS OR ROUNDED
(NOT RECOMMENDED)   CORNERS SQUARE FLUE

Figure 5-9   Types of flue liners

5.4 Effective Flue Area, EFA

5.4.1 Square Flues

For a square flue having a smooth surface, the effective flue area, EFA, is the same as that of a smooth, round flue with an internal diameter equal to the dimension of one side of the square. Thus, the four cross-hatched corners in figures 5-10 and 5-11 are inactive insofar as draft is concerned and their total area represents 21.5% of the total internal area B^2. The effective flue area, EFA, is represented by the circle having D for diameter and tangent to all four walls of the flue·

$$\text{Since } D = B; \text{ EFA} = 0.785B^2 \cong 0.8\ B^2$$

NOTE: See Table 5-A for effective flue area, EFA

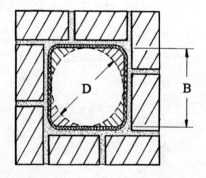

Figure 5-10   Effective square flue area

5.4.2   Rectangular Flues

The effective flue area, EFA, of a rectangular flue is the summation of the area of the half circle inscribed tangent to each end, plus the area of the rectangle between them. The diameter of the inscribed circle is D, which is the same as width B.

The area of the circle is $= 0.785D^2 = 0.785B^2 \cong 0.8\ B^2$

The area of the rectangle

is $= (A-D) \times B = (A-B)B$

The effective flue area, EFA

is $= 0.785B^2 + (A-B)B \cong 0.8\ B^2 + (A-B)B$

NOTE: See Table 5-A for effective flue area, EFA.

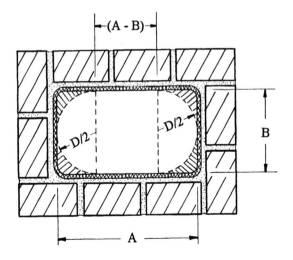

Figure 5-11   Effective rectangular flue area

99

5.5   *Effective Flue Area Requirements*

The area of the fireplace opening is multiplied by the flue area ratio to obtain the minimum required effective flue area.

The size of the flue lining selected should be equal to or larger than the required computed area.

PROBLEM: Determine the flue required for a single face 44" (1118 mm) wide and 28" (711 mm) fireplace with a chimney 18 ft. (5.5 m).

SOLUTION: The chimney is in excess of 15 ft. (4.6 m) from the smoke shelf to the top of the flue, therefore the effective area of the flue should be at least $\frac{1}{10}$ the area of the fireplace opening.

1.   Locate, on Figure 5-13, the intersection of 44" (1118 mm) width and 28" (711 mm) height on the graph.
2.   Read 125 sq.in. (0.08 m^2) effective flue area required.
3.   Select from Table 5-A 133 to 140 sq. in. (0.085 to 0.09 m^2) category, 10" x 11" (254 mm x 279 mm) flue lining.

PROBLEM: Determine flue size considering the height of the fireplace chimney 13 ft. (5.5 m) for the above example.

SOLUTION: The chimney is less than 15 ft. (4.6 m) high therefore the effective area of the flue should be at least $\frac{1}{8}$ the area of the fireplace opening.

1.   Locate on Figure 5-14 the intersection of 44" (1118 mm) width and 28" (0.71 m) height on the graph.
2.   Read 155 sq.in. (0.10 m^2) effective flue area required.
3.   Select from Table 5-A 13" x 14" (330 mm x 356 mm) flue.

The consideration of height allows a slight reduction in flue size

Chimney height is measured from the throat to the top of the chimney

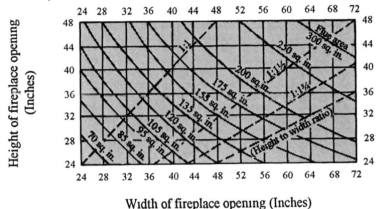

Width of fireplace opening (Inches)

Figure 5-12   Graph to determine area of flue for $^1/_{10}$ fireplace opening

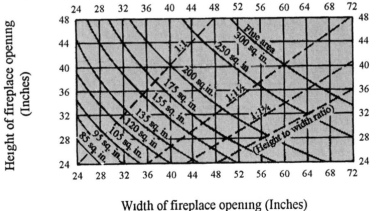

Width of fireplace opening (Inches)

Figure 5-13   Graph to determine area of flue for $^1/_8$ fireplace opening

Table 5-A Effective Area and Flue Sizes

Effective Area of Flue Lining	Nominal Flue Size	Actual Outside Dimensions	Inside Dimensions
Sq. In.	Inches	Inches	Inches
74	*8 x 13 SQ.	$9^{1}/_{8}$ x $13\frac{1}{2}$	$7\frac{1}{2}$ x $11\frac{1}{2}$
79	*$11\frac{1}{2}$ x $11\frac{1}{2}$ SQ	$11^{5}/_{8}$ x $11^{5}/_{8}$	10 x 10
83	+13 x 13 RC	13 x 13	$10\frac{1}{2}$ x $10\frac{1}{2}$
85	+$8\frac{1}{2}$ x 17 RC	$8\frac{1}{2}$ x 17	$6\frac{1}{4}$ x $14^{7}/_{8}$
85	+10 x 14 RC	$10\frac{1}{2}$ x $14\frac{3}{4}$	8 x $12^{3}/_{8}$
91	*8 x 13 OV	$8\frac{1}{4}$ x $12\frac{3}{4}$	$6\frac{1}{2}$ x $11\frac{1}{2}$
92	*8 x 17 SQ	$8\frac{3}{4}$ x $17^{5}/_{8}$	$6\frac{1}{2}$ x $15\frac{1}{2}$
92	+8 x $19\frac{1}{2}$ OV	8 x $19\frac{1}{2}$	$5\frac{3}{4}$ x $17\frac{1}{4}$
95	*8 x 17 OV	$8\frac{3}{4}$ x $17\frac{1}{4}$	$6\frac{3}{4}$ x $15\frac{1}{2}$
95	*11 RD	13	11
95	+10 x $17\frac{1}{2}$ RC	$9^{5}/_{8}$ x $17\frac{3}{4}$	7 x $15^{1}/_{8}$
99	+13 x 13 SQ	$13\frac{1}{4}$ x $13\frac{1}{4}$	$11\frac{1}{4}$ x $11\frac{1}{4}$
104	*8 x 19 OV	$8\frac{1}{2}$ x $19\frac{1}{2}$	$6\frac{1}{2}$ x $17^{3}/_{8}$
106	*8 x 20 SQ	$8^{3}/_{8}$ x $20\frac{1}{4}$	$6\frac{1}{4}$ x $18\frac{1}{4}$
113	*12 RD	$13\frac{1}{2}$	12
114	+12 x 16 SQ	12 x 16	$9\frac{3}{4}$ x $13\frac{3}{4}$
118	*10 x 17 OV	$10\frac{1}{4}$ x $18\frac{1}{4}$	8 x $16^{3}/_{8}$
119	*12 x 16 SQ	12 x 16	$10\frac{1}{2}$ x $10\frac{1}{2}$
126	+13 x 17 RC	13 x 17	$10\frac{1}{2}$ x $14\frac{1}{4}$
131	*13 x 17 OV	13 x 17	$10\frac{1}{2}$ x 14 $\frac{3}{4}$
136	*13 x 17 SQ	$12^{7}/_{8}$ x $17\frac{1}{2}$	$10\frac{1}{2}$ x $15\frac{1}{4}$
150	*13 x 18 OV	13 x 18	$10\frac{1}{4}$ x $17\frac{1}{4}$
154	+13 x 20 RC	13 x 20	$10\frac{1}{2}$ x $16\frac{1}{2}$
154	*16 x 16 SQ	16 x 16	14 x 14
160	+17 x 17 RC	17 x 17	$14\frac{1}{4}$ x $14\frac{1}{4}$
171	*17 x 17 OV	$17\frac{1}{4}$ x $17\frac{1}{4}$	$14\frac{3}{4}$ x $14\frac{3}{4}$
177	*15 RD	17	15
184	*13 x 21 OV	$13\frac{1}{4}$ x $22\frac{1}{4}$	$10\frac{1}{2}$ x $19\frac{3}{4}$
201	+17 x 20 RC	17 x $19\frac{3}{4}$	$14\frac{1}{2}$ x 17
201	*18 x18 SQ	18 x 18	16 x 16
210	*16 x 20 SQ	16 x 20	14 x 18

Table 5-A Effective Area and Flue Sizes (Continue)

246	*17 x 21 OV	17 $^5/_8$ x 22	15 x 18 $^5/_8$
254	+21 x 20 RC	21 x 20	18½ x 17 $^1/_8$
255	* 16 RD	18	16
255	*20 x 20 SQ	20 x 20	18 x 18
284	*21 x 21 OV	2 x 22	19 x 19
327	*20 x 24 OV	20 x 24	·18 x 22
346	*19 RD	21	19

NOTE   By industry convention, rectangular flues are designated by exterior dimension, round flues by interior diameter

NOTE   For dimensions in mm, multiply inches by 25 4
For are in sq mm multiply, sq in by 645 2

OV = OVAL, SQ = SQUARE, RC = ROUND CORNER, RD = ROUND

* CLAY FLUE LININGS, $^7/_8$ inch thick   These meet or exceed requirements of ASTM C 315
+ CONCRETE FLUE LININGS   These meet or exceed requirements of FHA, MPS 4900 1 Sec 604-6 7, ICBO Research Recommendation No 2602, City of Los Angles Research Report No 23878 Approximate wall thickness 1-$^1/_8$± (29 mm ±)
Check with local supplier for availability of flue liner sizes   It would be recommended to use a larger flue rather than a smaller flue if the proper size is not available

5.5.1   Effect of chimney height on flue size

It is good practice and the FHA requires that if the chimney is less than 15 ft (4 5 m) high, use $^1/_8$ ratio, if chimney is 15 ft (4 6 m) or more in height use $^1/_{10}$ ratio

5.5.2   Very large flues

For larger fireplaces that require very large flue area, rather than using two flue liners in a chimney, many times the flue is left unlined with 8 inches (203 mm) masonry walls   Unlined flues must have a minimum area of $^1/_8$ fireplace opening

5.6 Fireplace Openings and Required Flue Sizes

Table 5-B — Fireplace Openings and Required Flue Sizes

Type of Fireplace	Width of Opening W	Height of Opening H	Depth of Opening D	Area of Fireplace Opening for Flue Determination	Flue Size Required at $\frac{1}{10}$ Area of Fireplace Opening	Flue Size Required at $\frac{1}{8}$ Area of Fireplace Opening *(FHA requirements)
	Inches	Inches	Inches	Sq. In.	Inches x Inches	Inches x Inches
	28	24	20	672	8x13 sq	12x12 sq
	30	24	20	720	8x13 sq	8x17 sq
	30	26	20	780	12x12 sq	12¾ Rd
	36	26	20	936	8 x 17 ov	13x13 sq
	36	28	22	1008	9x19 ov	10x21 rc
	40	28	22	1120	10x21 rc	13x17 rc
	48	32	25	1536	13x20 rc	17x17 ov
	60	32	25	1920	17x17 ov	17x20 rc
	34	27	23	1107	10x21 rc	12x16 sq
	39	27	23	1223	12x16 sq	13x20 rc
	46	27	23	1388	12x16 sq	13x20 rc
	52	30	27	1884	17x17 ov	17x20 rc
	64	30	27	2085	17x20 rc	21x20 rc

Table 5-B — Fireplace Openings and Required Flue Sizes (Continued)

Type of Fireplace	Width of Opening W	Height of Opening H	Depth of Opening D	Area of Fireplace Opening for Flue Determination	Flue Size Required at $1/10$ Area of Fireplace Opening	Flue Size Required at $1/8$ Area of Fireplace Opening *(FHA Requirements)
	Inches	Inches	Inches	Sq. In.	Inches x Inches	Inches x Inches
	32	21	30	1344	10x21 rc.	13x20 rc.
	35	21	30	1470	13x17 rc.	17x17 ov.
	42	21	30	1764	13x20 rc.	17x20 rc.
	48	21	34	2016	17x17 rc.	17x21 ov.
	39	21	30	1638	13x20 rc.	17x17 rc.
	46	21	30	1932	17x17 ov.	17x20 ov.
	52	21	34	2184	17x20 ov.	21x20 rc.
	43	27	23	1782	13x21 ov.	17x20 rc.
	50	27	23	1971	17x17 ov.	17x21 ov.
	56	30	27	2490	17x21 ov.	21x21 ov.
	68	30	27	2850	21x21 ov.	**2-13x21 ov.

*FHA Requirement if chimney is less than 15 ft. (4.6 m) high, use $1/8$ ratio, if chimney is 15 ft. (4.6 m) or more in height use $1/10$ ratio.

**Rather than using two flue liners in chimney, many times the flue is left unlined with 8 inches (203 mm) masonry walls. Unlined flues must have a minimum area of $1/8$ fireplace opening.

5.7   *Flue Construction*

The flue should have a smooth, unobstructed passage for proper draft and smoke exhaustion. Flues may be lined with clay flue linings that are smooth and conform to ASTM C-315 or concrete flue liners conforming to ICBO R.R. No. 2602 or approved equivalent. Flue linings should extend at least 2 inches (51 mm) above the chimney cap. Available flue lining sizes are given in Tables 5-A.

If the required area of flue is very large and two flue liners would be required to satisfy the requirement, it may be more economical not to use two liners, but to use 8-inch (203 mm) thick masonry chimney walls, thus creating an unlined flue.

For FHA requirements and for unlined flues, the area required for the flue is one-eighth of the area of the fireplace opening. This is to allow for any possible irregularity of the flue surface.

Fireplaces with unusual openings or design, such as oval, round, triangular, etc., will have the size of the flue opening determined by the area of the fireplace opening. The proper coefficient should be used.

5.7.1   *Flue Liners*

Flue liners shall be supported on all sides. This can be accomplished by slushing with mortar or by placing brick or block adjacent to the flue for support. These support brick or block must be securely attached to the chimney. The flue liner should be supported but allowed to move vertically and expand with heat. This can be done by wrapping the flue liner with Koawool to keep the grout from bonding to the liner and provide space for thermal movement.

5.8   *Wide Chimneys*

Chimneys enhance the architecture of a home. Chimneys with various designs of width and shapes and various materials of stone, brick or block help beautify the total exterior of a home.

A chimney gives a feeling of substance, stability and permanence to a home. It is like a cornerpost and part of the foundation of the home.

The width of a fireplace often extends the full height to the top of the chimney. Thus, a wide chimney will have a the single flue which can be located anywhere within the width of the chimney. Consideration must be given to the reinforcement and anchorage of the extra width of the chimney to withstand wind and earthquake forces.

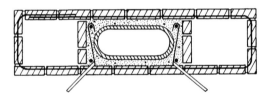

Figure 5-14   Wide chimney with flue located in center

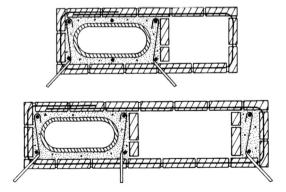

Figure 5-15   Wide chimney with flue located to side

5.9   Multiple Flue Chimneys

All fireplaces must have individual flues. This rule must be followed even if two fireplaces are next to each other and facing in adjacent rooms (Figure 5-16); however, flues may be enclosed in a common chimney (Figures 5-16 and 5-17).

Adjacent flues should be separated with four inches (102 mm) of tempered mortar or grout filling between the flue liners. If adjacent flues are not separated and surrounded by mortar or grout, the joints in adjoining flues should be staggered. FHA requires that when more than two flues are located in the same chimney, a four inch (102 mm) wythe bonded into the chimney must be installed, separating flues in a chimney. It may be desirable to slope one flue towards the other flue to reduce the width of the chimney. Flue lining should be accurately cut on an angle to fit the slope.

Many times an outdoor barbecue fireplace is connected into the chimney of an indoor fireplace. Even in this case, the barbecue and the fireplace must each have its own flue.

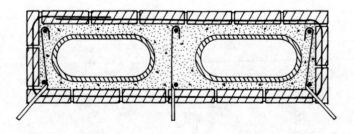

Figure 5-16   Wide chimney with two flues

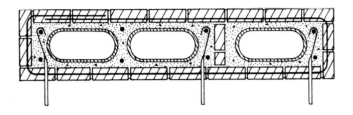

Figure 5-17   Wide chimney with three flues

The pouring or spilling of smoke from one flue to an adjacent flue occurs where downdraft from interior suction or vertical wind currents force smoke down an inactive flue as it exhausts from the adjoining flue. This can be prevented with flues of different heights above the masonry as shown in Figure 5-18 and also by the use of chimney caps and wall separations between flues.

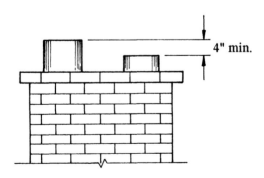

Figure 5-18   Vary the elevation of the top of flue

109

5.10   Reinforcing Chimneys and Fireplaces

5.10.1   Chimney Reinforcement

Every chimney in Seismic Zones 2, 3 and 4 and in areas of high winds such as hurricanes and tornadoes shall be reinforced with at least four ½ inch (13 mm) diameter vertical reinforcing bars. The bars shall extend the full height of the chimney.

The vertical bars shall have a minimum cover of ½ inch (13 mm) of grout or mortar tempered to a pouring consistency.

Vertical bars may be spliced with a 20 inch (508 mm) lap if permitted by local building department. The bars shall be tied horizontally at 18 inch (457 mm) maximum intervals with not less than ¼ inch (6 mm) diameter steel tie at each interval.

Two ties shall also be provided at the bend in a bar where it changes from a sloped position to a vertical position. Maximum slope of vertical steel should be six inch (152 mm) horizontal to twelve inch (305 mm) vertical.

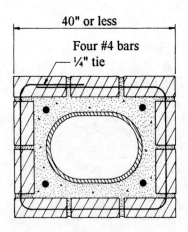

40" or less

Four #4 bars
¼" tie

Figure 5-19   Vertical reinforcing and ties in small chimney

Where the width of the chimney exceeds 40 inches (1016 mm), two additional ½ inch (13 mm) diameter vertical bars shall be provided for each additional flue incorporated into the chimney or for each additional 40 inches (1016 mm) in width or fraction thereof.

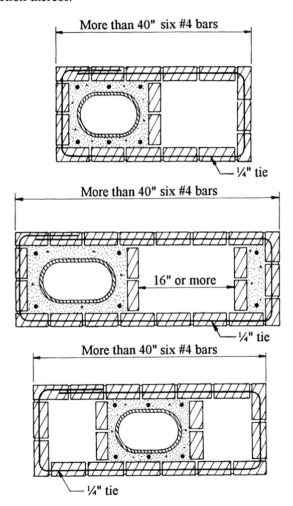

Figure 5-20   Vertical reinforcing and ties in a wide chimney with one flue

The above reinforcement requirement will be adequate for chimneys to twelve feet (3.7 m) above anchor tie.

Chimneys of excessive height, weight, width or other special or unusual features should be designed in accordance with sound engineering principles to withstand the forces imposed by wind or earthquake.

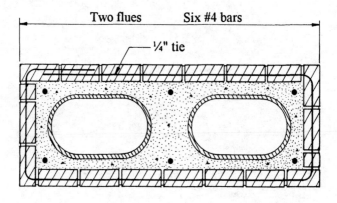

Figure 5-21   Vertical reinforcing and ties in a wide chimney with two flues

5.10.2   *Fireplace Reinforcement*

It has been very evident that not only must chimneys be reinforced, but fire boxes must also be properly reinforced.

In the Whittier earthquakes of Oct. 1 and 4, 1987 and the Northridge earthquake of January 17, 1994 some fire boxes and chimneys were severely damaged even though the chimneys were reinforced. Inspection revealed lack of ties or proper fastening of anchor straps to the roof or floor diaphragm.

The Uniform Building Code details the requirements of vertical and horizontal reinforcement in the chimney and around the firebox

The following provisions of the 1994 UBC Section 3102 4 3 requirements for "Reinforcing and Seismic Anchorage" apply in Seismic Zones 2, 3 and 4

a.   The bars shall extend the full height of the chimney.

b.   Bars shall be spliced in accordance with the applicable requirements of Chapter 19 or 21.

c.   The vertical bars shall have a minimum cover of ½ inch (13 mm) of grout or mortar.

d.   The bars shall be tied horizontally at 18-inch (457 mm) intervals with not less than ¼-inch-diameter (6.4 mm) steel ties.

e.   The slope of the inclined portion of the offset in vertical bars shall not exceed 2 units vertical in 1 unit horizontal.

f.   Two ties shall also be placed at each bend in vertical bars.

g.   Where the width of the chimney exceeds 40 inches (1016 mm), two additional #4 vertical bars shall be provided for each additional flue incorporated in the chimney or for each additional 40 inches (1016 mm) in width or fraction thereof.

In the County of Los Angeles, California, it is required that the firebox shall have additional vertical and horizontal steel as follows:

Vertical bars

a   No. 4 reinforcing bars shall be hooked in the footing

b.   Bars shall be at each corner and spaced not more than 24 inches (610 mm) on center around the chimney.

c.   Continuous for the full height of the chimney at the corners and between flues and other bars terminating 36 inches (915 mm) above the level of the smoke shelves where a reduction in the size of the chimney permits the omission of the bars.

EXCEPTION: Chimneys constructed of hollow-unit masonry may have vertical reinforcement spliced to footing dowels providing that the splice is inspected prior to grouting of the wall.

Horizontal bars

a.   Horizontal steel ties shall be ¼ inch (6 mm) diameter

b.   Ties shall be looped around vertical reinforcement

c   Ties shall be spaced not more than 12 inches (305 mm) on center except that two ¼ inch (6 mm) ties or one No 3 tie may be spaced at not more than 24 inches (610 mm) on center.

d.   Two ¼ inch (6 mm) ties or one No. 3 tie shall be placed adjacent to the steel seismic anchor straps.

5.10.3   *Arrangement of Reinforcing Steel*

The following figures show possible arrangements of reinforcing steel for various types of fireplaces and chimneys.

5.10.3.1   *Fireplace with One Center Opening*

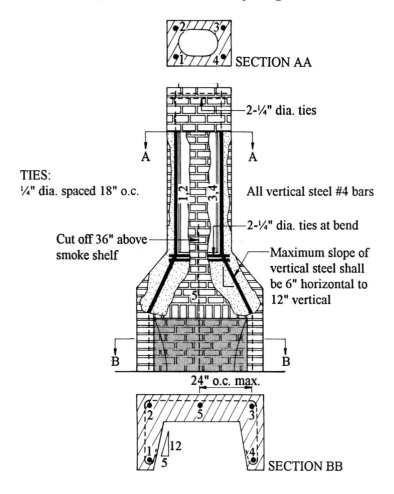

Figure 5-22   Arrangement of reinforcing steel in fireplace with one opening

5.10.3.2 Fireplace with Offset Chimney

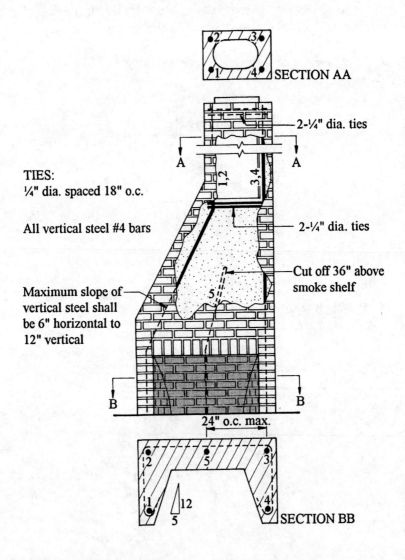

SECTION AA

2-¼" dia. ties

A   A

TIES:
¼" dia. spaced 18" o.c.

All vertical steel #4 bars

2-¼" dia. ties

Cut off 36" above smoke shelf

Maximum slope of vertical steel shall be 6" horizontal to 12" vertical

B   B

24" o.c. max.

12
5

SECTION BB

Figure 5-23   Arrangement of reinforcing steel in fireplace with offset chimney

5.10.3.3 *Fireplace with Straight Up Chimney*

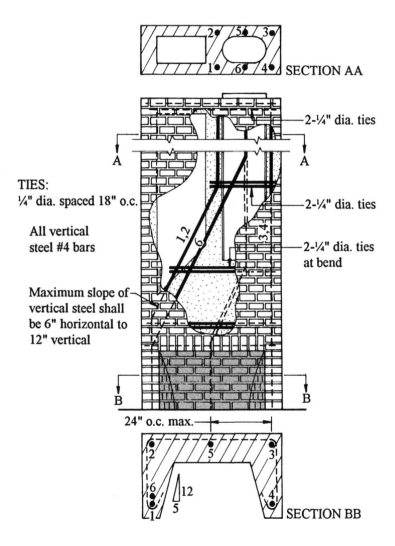

Figure 5-24   Arrangement of reinforcing steel in fireplace with a straight up chimney

5.10.3.4 Fireplace with Wide Straight Up Chimney

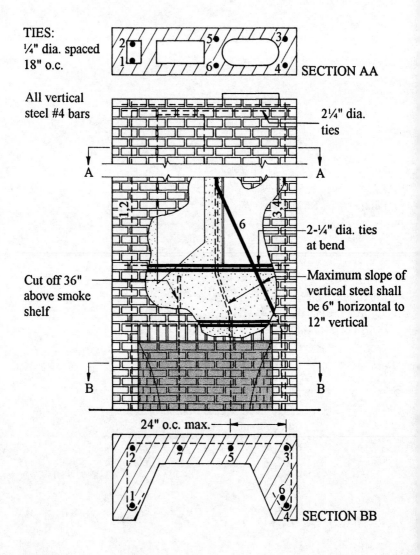

TIES:
¼" dia. spaced
18" o.c.

SECTION AA

All vertical
steel #4 bars

2¼" dia.
ties

2-¼" dia. ties
at bend

Cut off 36"
above smoke
shelf

Maximum slope of
vertical steel shall
be 6" horizontal to
12" vertical

24" o.c. max.

SECTION BB

Figure 5-25   Arrangement of reinforcing steel in fireplace
with a wide straight up chimney

5.10.3.5 Corner Fireplace

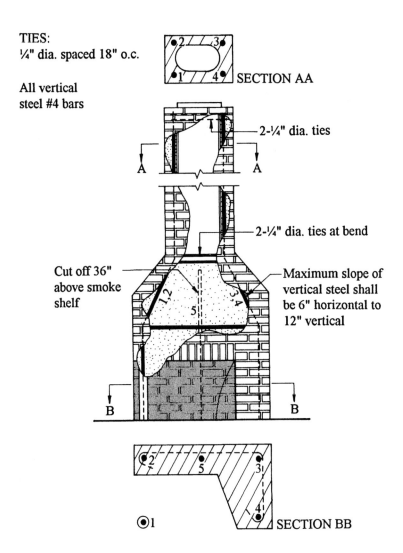

TIES:
¼" dia. spaced 18" o.c.

All vertical
steel #4 bars

SECTION AA

2-¼" dia. ties

2-¼" dia. ties at bend

Cut off 36"
above smoke
shelf

Maximum slope of
vertical steel shall
be 6" horizontal to
12" vertical

SECTION BB

Figure 5-26   Arrangement of reinforcing steel in a corner or "L" fireplace

119

5.10.3.6 Fireplace Open on Three Sides

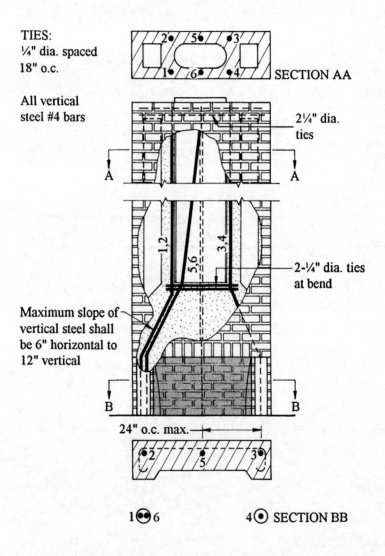

TIES:
¼" dia. spaced
18" o.c.

SECTION AA

All vertical
steel #4 bars

2¼" dia.
ties

2-¼" dia. ties
at bend

Maximum slope of
vertical steel shall
be 6" horizontal to
12" vertical

24" o.c. max.

1 ●● 6   4 ⊙ SECTION BB

Figure 5-27   Arrangement of reinforcing bars in fireplace open on three sides

5.11   Anchorage of Chimney to Building

It is required by all codes to provide anchor straps from the chimney to the building when the chimney is outside the building and against the exterior wall.

For a standard size chimney with one flue, steel straps approximately $^3/_{16}$ inch by 1 inch (5 mm x 25 mm), or standard FHA anchors, are embedded in the grout and around the reinforcing steel. They are attached with two $^1/_2$ inch (13 mm) bolts or four $^3/_8$ inch (10 mm) diameter by three inch (76 mm) lag screws to framing members. Bolts or lag screws used in all anchors must each be in separate holes. Blocking between rafters is recommended to provide diaphragm resistance.

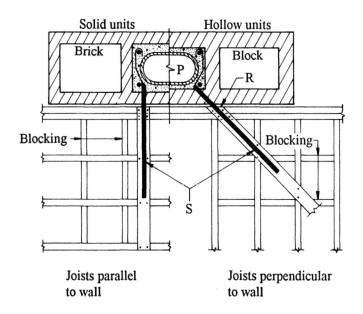

Figure 5-28   Anchorage of small chimney

Where the joists do not head into the chimney, the anchor straps are connected to two inch by four inch (51 mm x 102 mm) ties crossing a minimum of four joists. The ties shall be connected to each joist with two 16d nails. *As an alternative to the two inch by four inch (51 mm x 102 mm) ties, the straps shall be connected to the structural framework by two ½ inch (13 mm) bolts in an approved manner.* Where the two inch by four inch (51 mm x 102 mm) tie is installed at the floor line, it is necessary to notch the floor joists. This is undesirable. This allows an unspecified alternative connection, but requires the connections to be made by bolts.

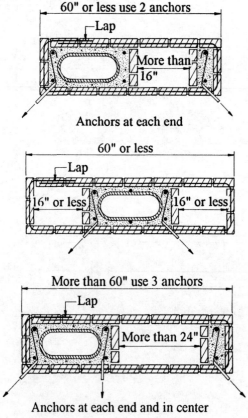

Figure 5-29   Anchorage of wide chimneys

When plates are cut, anchor the chimney with $^3/_{16}$ inch by one inch (5 mm x 25 mm) steel straps hooked into the chimney and attached to plates by two $^1/_2$ inch by four inch (13 mm x 102 mm) lag screws or two $^1/_2$ inch (13 mm) bolts.

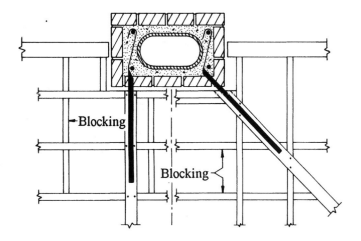

Figure 5-30   Bond beam and cut plate anchorage

When the chimney is two stories high, it should be anchored at both the second floor and at the ceiling or roof level. Many times, when a chimney extends considerably above the roof level, an intermediate lateral support or tie may be placed between the roof line and the top of the chimney and tied back to the roof.

If a chimney is inside a house, passes through the roof and is completely surrounded by roof diaphragm, generally no special anchors need be provided. The chimney would be supported by the roof diaphragm in the event it is subjected to lateral forces; however, some codes may require steel anchors even for chimneys completely surrounded by the roof or floor diaphragm. Check local codes for this requirement.

5.11.1 Anchor Tie Connection Requirements for Tall Chimneys

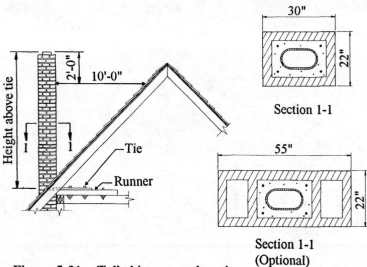

Figure 5-31   Tall chimney anchor ties

Table 5-C   Anchor Tie Connection Requirements for Tall Chimney

Height of Chimney Above Tie	Small Chimney Approx. 22" x 30" (559 mm x 762 mm)		Wide Straight Up Chimney Approx. 22" x 55" (559 mm x 1397 mm)	
	Inches (mm) Bolt Tie 2" x 4" (51 x 102 mm) to Runner 2 ties	Nail 2" x 4" (51 x 102 mm) Runner to Rafters or Joists 2 ties	Inches (mm) Bolt Tie 2" x 4" (51 x 102 mm) to Runner 3 ties	Nail 2" x 4" (51 x 102 mm) Runner to Rafters or Joists 3 ties
10 ft (3.0 m)	4 -½" (2-13 mm) bolts	8-16d nails 4 Members	4 -½" (2-13 mm) bolts	8-16d nails 4 Members
12 ft (3.7 m)	4 -½" (2-13 mm) bolts	8-16d nails 4 Members	or 4 -½" (4-13 mm) bolts	8-16d nails 4 Members

Use only 16d common nails.

5.11.2   *Anchor Tie Connection Requirements for Gable Ceiling*

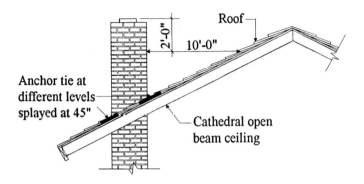

Figure 5-32   Anchor tie connection for gable end open beam ceiling

5.12   *Corbeled Chimneys*

Corbeling is projecting masonry from the plane of the wall or fireplace by small distances for each course of masonry. Fireplace chimneys may be corbeled when necessary, but not more than 4 inches (102 mm) in each 24 inches (610 mm) in height, with a maximum corbeling of not more than one-third of the dimension of the chimney in the direction of the corbeling. Architectural corbeling should be detailed on plans.

Note: A chimney may be corbeled more than one third of its dimension provided it is engineered to accommodate the eccentric loads and stresses. The calculations can be provided by a professional engineer.

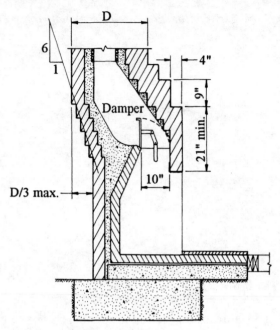

Figure 5-33   Corbeled chimney

5.13   Height of Chimney

To prevent the upward draft from being neutralized by downward eddies from neighboring roofs, the chimney flue should be built at least 4 feet (1.2 m) above flat or semi-flat roofs and two feet (0.6 m) above the ridge of pitched roofs. The top of the chimney above the roof must be two feet (0.6 m) above any point on the roof within ten feet (3.0 m) of the chimney.

Consideration should also be given to the effect of smoke emitting from the chimney and whether it will be blown into windows of the building adjacent structures. Although the buildings may be ten feet (3.0 m) or more away, this consideration should be evaluated to insure that a nuisance is not increased.

In the event that a fireplace does not draw well or smokes, it may be remedied by increasing the height of the chimney, thus improving the draft.   An increase of several feet (meters) will cause a significant improvement in the draft.

At elevations above 2,000 feet (610 m), the chimney height should be raised slightly or the flue area should be increased and the height of the fireplace opening should be decreased. A rough rule-of-thumb is to increase both height and cross-sectional area of the flue about five percent for each 1,000 feet (305 m) above sea level.

Tall chimney provides clearance from steep roof

5.14   Fireplaces on Two or More Floors

Many times a fireplace is located in the living room and immediately above it, in the master bedroom, is another fireplace. Or, in apartment buildings, there can be fireplaces above each other and thus multiple flues in a chimney are required. Each fireplace must have a separate flue.

Figure 5-35 shows a way to combine multi-level fireplaces in one chimney. Note that each flue takes off properly from the center of the smoke chamber.

The top of the flue should have a height difference of at least four inches (102 mm) and as much as twelve inches (305 mm) to prevent smoke from pouring from one flue into the other flue. The flue for the fireplace on the upper floor should be higher than the flue of the fireplace on the lower floor.

Chimney with fireplaces on both floors

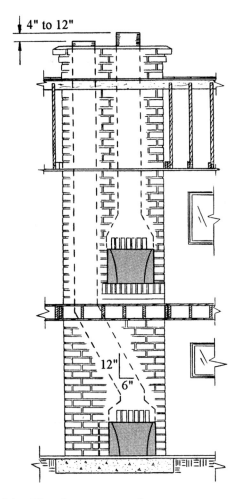

Figure 5-34   Fireplaces on two floors

5.15   *Flue Offset*

Masonry flues may be offset at a slope of not more than twelve inches (305 mm) horizontal to 24 inches (610 mm) vertical. The maximum total offset shall not be more than one-third the dimension of the chimney, where the chimney is in the direction of the offset unless supplementary support is provided. The slope of the transition from the fireplace to the flue shall not exceed one inch (25 mm) horizontal in two inches (51 mm) vertical.

5.16   *Spark Arrester*

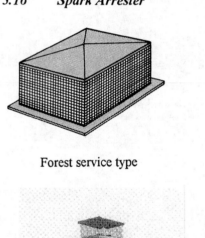

Forest service type   Flat type

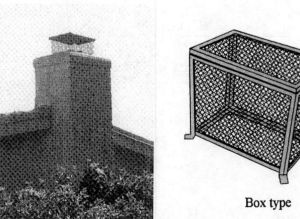

Box type

Figure 5-35   Spark arresters

Spark arresters are required in wooded areas and should be used in all chimneys, they prevent hot cinders or fiery brands from leaving the chimney and falling on a roof, which may cause the roof to start on fire.

The spark arrester screens, $1/2$ inch (13 mm) mesh, are open enough not to obstruct the draft but will prevent cinders and paper from flying out of the chimney. The flat type fits on top of or inside the flue liner and the box type fits over the top of the flue. The box type allows more air to pass through. In forested or wooded areas the spark arrester screen should have a metal cap to prevent heat from going straight up.

FROM UBC CHAPTER 31

3102.3.8 Spark arrester. Where determined necessary by the building official due to local climatic conditions or where sparks escaping from the chimney would create a hazard, chimneys attached to any appliance or fireplace that burns solid fuel shall be equipped with an approved spark arrester. The net free area of the spark arrester shall not be less than four times the net free area of the outlet of the chimney.

Chimneys used with fireplaces or heating appliances in which solid or liquid fuel is used shall be provided with a spark arrester as required in the Fire Code.

EXCEPTION: Chimneys which are located more than 200 feet (60 960 mm) from any mountainous, brush-covered or forest-covered land or land covered with flammable material and are not attached to a structure having less than a Class C roof covering, as set forth in Chapter 15.

5.17   *Chimney Cap*

Every masonry chimney should have a chimney cap to terminate the brick and protect the chimney. This cap can be precast concrete, cast in place concrete or a mortar cap.

A weather cap sheds water from the liner and casing at the top of a chimney. A cracked cap or one in which the mortar joints have deteriorated can allow moisture penetration into the casing of a masonry chimney. If the temperature of the masonry drops below freezing when the fireplace is not in use, and rises above freezing during use, the freeze-thaw action may cause spalling and eventual disintegration of the masonry.

The chimney cap shall extend to the exterior face of the masonry or beyond so as to prevent moisture penetration from the top of the masonry wall and shed the water away from the flue.

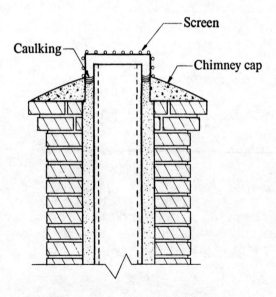

Figure 5-36   Mortar or concrete chimney cap

5.18   Chimney Hood Flue Cap

The surrounding outdoor area around the chimney may have a significant influence on the performance of the fireplace. A hill, bluff, tall trees or high buildings nearby can cause air flow patterns that could prevent the chimney from drawing properly. This could create downdrafts that will cause smoke to pour into the room.

To reduce the possibility of downdraft, cover the top of the flue with a chimney hood so that the wind will blow over the top of the flue and not directly into it. The chimney hood should be open on at least two sides, and the open area on one side must be larger than the flue area.

A simple hood can be made of concrete or steel and secured to the top of the chimney. The chimney hood also protects the flue and fireplace from rain and snow.

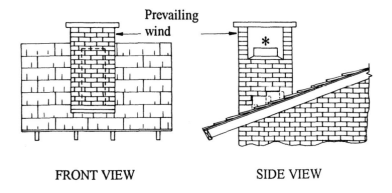

FRONT VIEW   SIDE VIEW

Figure 5-37   Hooded chimney helps draft

*This opening should be large so that the hood cap does not act as a cover for the flue, which could create a back pressure and reduce the draw of the flue.

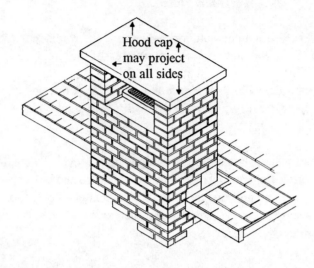

Figure 5-38   Chimney hoods improve appearance and prevent rain and snow from entering the chimney

Figure 5-39   Metal flue cap

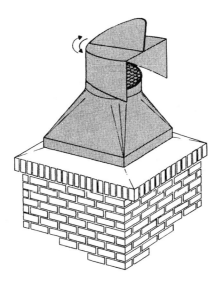

Figure 5-40   Directional metal flue hood

Many times, there is insufficient suction or draft up the chimney for good burning. In order to increase suction, a sheet metal directional flue hood placed on top of the chimney creates the reduced pressure at the top and thus improves the draft. Other similar types of devices may be used to increase draft or suction and thus improve performance of the fireplace.

5.18.1   Chimney Tops or Pots

The top of a chimney may be improved in appearance by the installation of a chimney top or pot. This ceramic device enhances a chimney, extends its height, provides a differential height to an adjacent flue and helps prevent downdrafts. The chimney top may be considered part of the chimney.

There are numerous styles that can be used depending on the design and architecture of the chimney and structure.

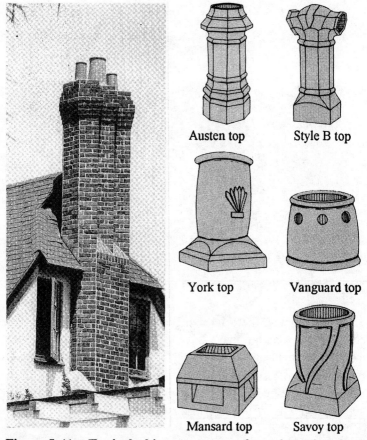

Austen top   Style B top

York top   Vanguard top

Mansard top   Savoy top

Figure 5-41 Typical chimney pots, a few of the hundreds available (Courtesy of Superior Clay Corp.)

5.18.2 Installation of a Chimney Top

The chimney top should be properly anchored to prevent it from blowing off in the event of a tornado or hurricane or shaking off due to an earthquake. A $^1/_2$ inch (13 mm) diameter hole should be drilled on opposite sides of the top and a $^1/_4$ inch (6.4 mm) or $^3/_8$ inch (9.5 mm) bar, 12 inch (305 mm) long used to anchor the top into the grout.

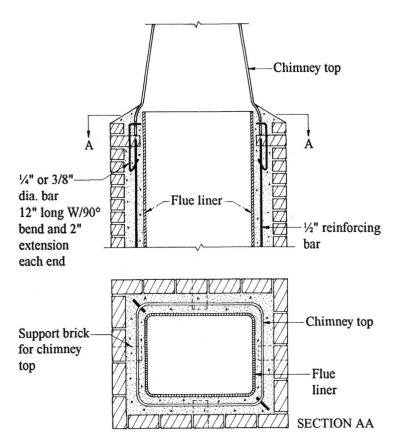

¼" or 3/8" dia. bar 12" long W/90° bend and 2" extension each end

Chimney top

Flue liner

½" reinforcing bar

Support brick for chimney top

Chimney top

Flue liner

SECTION AA

Figure 5-42   Security of chimney pot on top of chimney stack

5.19   *Chimney Flashing*

Water leakage around chimneys can be prevented by proper flashing at the intersection of chimney and roof. The connection should be made weather-tight by means of flashing and counter flashing of copper, rust-resistant metal or other approved material. It should be installed on the upper or high side of the chimney (see Figures 5-43 and 5-44) so it will deflect the water around the chimney.

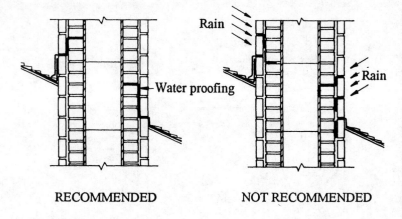

RECOMMENDED   NOT RECOMMENDED

Figure 5-43   Flashing of stone veneer over masonry chimney

When built-up roofing is used, flashing may be accomplished by mopping up the chimney side over a cant strip at the intersection. Counter flashing is required in this case and is bonded into the mortar joints and lapped down over the flashing so that water runs over rather than into any seams.

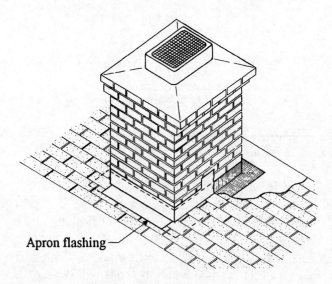

Figure 5-44   Flashing around chimney

138

Base flashing and counter flashing are installed at the chimney/roof interface. The base flashing is installed first on the face of the chimney perpendicular to the ridge line with tabs at each corner. The flashing shall extend a minimum of four inches (102 mm) up the face of the chimney and along the roof.

Counter flashing is then installed over the base flashing. It is inserted into a mortar joint for ¾ inch to one inch (19 mm to 25 mm) and mortared solidly into the joint. The counter flashing shall lap the base flashing by at least three inches (76 mm).

If the flashing is installed in sections, the flashing higher up the roof line shall lap over the lower flashing a minimum of two inches (51 mm).

All joints in the base flashing and counter flashing shall be thoroughly sealed. The unexposed side of any bends in the flashing shall also be sealed.

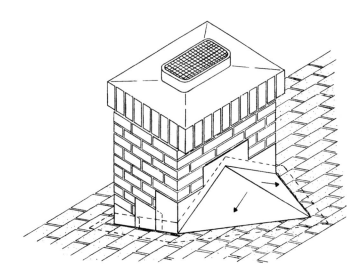

Figure 5-45   Flashing cricket at chimney

5.20   Prefabricated Metal Flues

After the Northridge Earthquake in Southern California on January 17, 1994, the City of Los Angeles hurriedly passed an ordinance urging the use of prefabricated metal flues for chimneys to reduce weight. It is interesting to note that although a few masonry chimneys failed and fell over, the cause was mainly due to lack of proper anchorage of the chimney to the structure. In many instances, the ties were not nailed, screwed or bolted to the diaphragm and the chimney was in effect a free standing, cantilever element. Where the chimneys were properly reinforced, anchored and tied to the structure, they performed well.

However, the City of Los Angeles hastily acted on the condition of collapsed chimneys and accepted the use of factory-built chimney assemblies with a U.L. label for the reconstruction of residential chimneys. The City of Los Angeles Department of Building and Safety issued standard details to facilitate the installation of these metal flue chimneys but ignored the thousands of masonry chimneys that were not damaged and performed very well through the earthquake.

In order to show how the transition is made from a masonry fire box to a metal chimney, an adapter ring is set on top of a bond beam above the smoke chamber. This permits the installation of a factory-built U.L. approved chimney flue. The flue is enclosed in a chase framed with steel studs, or if permitted but not recommended, wood studs. Special attention must be given to insure proper clearance to combustible materials. The exterior sheathing and cement stucco plaster and thin brick veneer covering are installed as the final exterior finish.

For engineering calculations for masonry chimney, see Section 7.3.

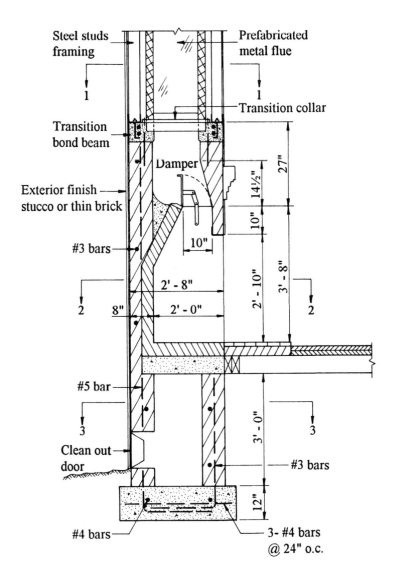

Figure 5-46   Cross-section of a metal flue chimney

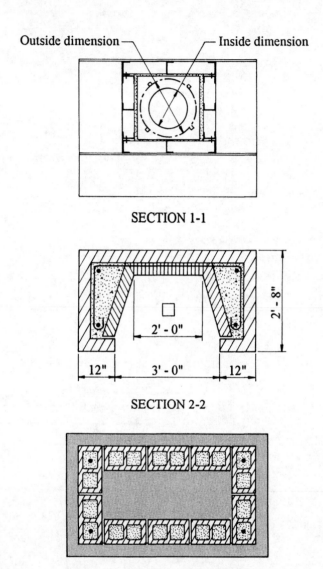

Outside dimension — Inside dimension

SECTION 1-1

2' - 8"

2' - 0"

12"   3' - 0"   12"

SECTION 2-2

SECTION 3-3

Figure 5-47   Sections of a metal flue chimney

FIREPLACE AND CHIMNEY
CARE AND OPERATION

6.1   Chimney Care

6.1.1   Inspection

To inspect a chimney, lower a light on a weighted extension cord. Look for loose or fallen bricks, cracks, or breaks in the flue lining. Check on the degree of soot build up. Inspect outside of chimney by prodding mortar joints with a knife to test for loose or crumbling mortar.

6.1.2   Cleaning

If the fireplace is used continuously, a thorough annual chimney cleansing is a must. A weighted sack stuffed with hay, or a scratchy brush, may be pulled up and down the flue to dislodge the accumulation of soot. *Important:* The front of the fireplace should be sealed off while the chimney is being cleaned, otherwise soot will flow into the room. By far the cleanest method is to have the flue vacuumed by professional chimney cleaners.

Some chemical compounds are available for burning out the soot. Fire authorities recommend crystalline compounds as being best for this operation. If the soot accumulation is unusually heavy, however, it is probably more safely removed by mechanical means.

6.1.3   Chimney Fires

Although most chimneys will probably withstand the heat of a chimney fire, flames may pass through a crack into the walls, or burning flakes of soot may ignite the roof. If a chimney breaks into flame, the first step is to call the fire department. While waiting for the firemen, or if the fireplace is beyond fire service, it is helpful to throw salt or baking soda on the fire in the grate and douse the roof with a garden hose.

6.1.4   Reducing Creosote Build-up

Many gases are produced during wood combustion. If the temperature in the fireplace is not high enough, or if there is insufficient combustion air, these gases will not burn completely and may condense as creosote on the cool surfaces of the flue system. Creosote is liquid when formed initially, but as moisture and volatile liquids are driven off by further heating, it becomes tacky and may eventually form a hard, glazed coating. If not removed periodically, large quantities of creosote and soot can accumulate. Their ignition can result in a high temperature chimney fire that may last as long as 15-25 minutes, and that can subject the liner to dangerous temperatures above 1100°C (2000°F). The high temperature may present a fire risk to adjacent combustible material or may structurally weaken the chimney. During any creosote fire in a chimney, the residue may curl, peel off the walls and obstruct the flue passage. After any chimney fire, the chimney should be inspected to ensure that the flue passage is not obstructed, thermally distorted or otherwise damaged.

One method for reducing creosote build up is to gradually stoke a medium hot fire for 15 to 30 minutes, which tends to burn off the creosote in small amounts. Seasoned or dry wood will form less creosote deposits than unseasoned or wet wood. In mild weather, frequent slow burning of the fireplace will severely aggravate the creosote problem.

Creosote can never be entirely eliminated if wood is burned, but it can be minimized by using a high temperature fire to ensure that the maximum amount of gaseous products is burned before entering the vent system. The risk of a serious chimney fire can be minimized by careful scraping or brushing to remove any creosote or soot particles that have accumulated in the venting system.

Inspection of chimney flues is important, especially at the beginning of each heating season. By inspection, any problems can be found that may occur and correction measures taken. Inspect chimneys from the roof using a flashlight, or use a mirror in the cleanout to look up through the chimney flue. **Any time an inspection shows soot or creosote build-up, the chimney should be cleaned.**

6.1.5   Caution

The use of chemicals that are supposed to clean the chimney when placed on a fire could produce heat intense enough to cause damage and develop thermal stresses in the concrete masonry and clay flue liners that could contribute to deterioration.

6.1.6   Fire Safety

A chimney must protect any adjacent combustible material from the hot gases within it. The properties of cellulose-type materials, e.g. wood or paper, change when these materials are exposed to high temperatures for a long time. After such exposure, they may ignite at a temperature lower than that which would otherwise cause them only to char or discolor, thereby making a potential fire hazard difficult to detect. The maximum safe temperature for wood or other cellulose-type materials is about 90°C (200°F) following such exposure.

6.2   Tips for Safe Fireplace Operation

A fireplace fire, properly laid and fed, is easy to tend and trouble-free. Here is a good method for building a fire.

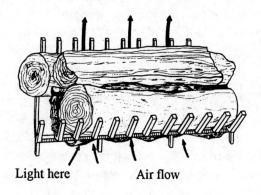

Light here   Air flow

Figure 6-1   Logs in a grate

1.   Use a steel grate or andirons to hold the wood or logs to obtain best results.

2.   Open damper to ensure proper operation.

3.   Crumple newspaper on the grate and lay in some kindling or small pieces of dry wood for starter. Then place three logs to the rear of the grate or andirons and light newspapers. Slightly open a window for air circulation if the house is well insulated. **Important:** Always use the three-log configuration for fast lighting and satisfactory burning.

4. Stack the logs so that the flames can get between them. Use larger logs when the fire is well established. Logs stacked in a teepee style allow improved circulation of air and more complete combustion, thus reducing pollution.

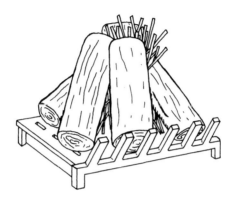

Figure 6-2   Logs Teepee Style

5. Keep glass door and screen closed when the fire is burning.

6. Close damper completely down only when the fire is completely out and ashes are cold. Keep damper closed when the fireplace is not in use to prevent unnecessary loss of heated or cooled air.

7. Slow burning hard woods make the best fuel. Green wood gives off less heat and can cause excess creosote to build up in the chimney.

8. When ashes build up under the grate, all but a base layer about one inch (25 mm) should be removed.

9. Never use a fireplace as an incinerator.

10. Never burn a Christmas tree in a fireplace.

6.3   Causes and Correction of a Smoking Fireplace

A fireplace that smokes may be a result of improper construction or design. The principal causes of smoking and the corrections are:

1.   Improper throat formation, leaving flat masonry ledges which obstruct the draft.
Correction: *Remove flat masonry ledges to clear throat areas.*

2.   Inadequate downdraft shelf and flue area.   Fireplace opening is too large for the flue.
Correction: *Decrease size of fireplace opening by installing a hood, or raise the hearth, or close in the sides.*

3.   The chimney top is lower than the highest point of the roof. Chimney is too short to provide draft.
Correction: *Increase the height of the chimney either by adding more masonry or by installing a chimney extension.*

4.   Improper location of the fireplace.
Correction: *Arrange furniture or provide a screen to change air flow, draft, characteristics in room.*

5.   The chimney is located within 30 feet (9.1 m) of higher buildings or trees, over which the prevailing winds blow, placing a pressure on top of the chimney, reducing the draft.
Correction: *Provide a hood on top of the chimney.*

6.   Tightly weather-stripped home which doesn't permit sufficient oxygen to keep fire burning properly and air is drawn down the chimney to interfere with the draft.
Correction: *Open a window two or three inches to provide air, or provide larger external air intake ports.*

7.   Improper location of flue above throat, allowing damper closure blade to swing back beneath the chimney flue beyond the inside vertical wall.

Correction: *Place a brick or other stop behind the damper blade to prevent it from opening beyond the inside vertical wall of the chimney.   Do not open damper all the way.*

8.   Opening too high and fireplace too shallow.

Correction: *Install a fireplace hood to increase the effective depth of the fireplace and decrease the height of the opening.*

9.   Flue choked by debris

Correction: *Debris generally lodges on the smoke shelf and may impede the working of the damper.   Remove the damper blade or valve plate and clean out the debris through the fireplace throat.   If the debris is lodged in the bend of the flue, dislodge with a pole or weighted line and remove from smoke shelf.*

6.4   Other Common Fireplace Problems

1.   Inadequate clearance from combustibles.

Make sure that proper clearances are maintained.   Minimum clearances are:

   a.   Two inches (51 mm) for external installed chimneys.
   b.   Two inches (51 mm) for chimneys built within the structure.
   c.   Six inches (152 mm) around the fireplace opening.
   d.   Sixteen inches (406 mm) minimum extension of the outer hearth, and at least eight inches (203 mm) to the sides of the fireplace opening, or
   If the fireplace opening is six square feet ($0.56 \ m^2$), or more,

  e.   Twenty inches (508 mm) minimum extension of the outer hearth, and at least twelve inches (305 mm) to the sides of the opening.

2.   Inadequate wall thickness.

The walls must be built to adequate thickness:

  a.   *Minimum thickness of firebrick in fireplace is 2 inches (51 mm), with some local building codes requiring 4 inches (102 mm) thickness.*
  b.   *Minimum thickness for unlined chimneys is eight inches (203 mm) and four inches (102 mm) for chimneys lined with an approved flue of at least $^5/_8$ inch (16 mm).*

3.   Poor liner joints.

During the construction process, it is important that the flues are mortared with refractory mortar to maintain the same properties as the flues. Care must also be taken to see that the flues are properly aligned with each other, and that the inside joints be finished to eliminate any irregularities that may interfere with the rising smoke.

4.   Separated fireplace face.

Design the face to be bonded or tied with wall ties.

5.   Improper support of hearths.

Code requires that the hearth be supported by non-combustible materials and this requirement must be strictly observed. Failure to do so may be the eventual cause of a catastrophic fire.

6.   Poor smoke chamber construction.

Care should be taken to see that the smoke chamber is smoothly finished and seals the flue lining on all four sides. Exercise caution where the damper meets the smoke chamber so that the damper can be easily and fully opened and closed. The smoke chamber should be no taller than the width of the fireplace opening and the walls should be inclined no more than 45° from the vertical.

7.   Improper clearance between the flue and chimney.

In multiple flue chimneys, the flues should be separated by at least a four inch (102 mm) wythe of masonry. Allow some room between the flue and chimney by slushing with mortar to allow for some expansion and contraction as the flue warms and cools.

8.   Poor crown construction.

The function of the chimney crown is to shed water. However, a crown that does not consider thermal movement at the flue will crack, allowing water to easily penetrate to the interior of the chimney. This moisture will cause rapid chimney deterioration. A precast crown is recommended.

9.   Improper chimney height.

For optimum performance, a chimney should be at least fifteen feet (4.6 m) in height, and the top must be at least two feet (0.6 m) taller than any structure within a ten foot (3.0 m) radius.

10.   Fireplace too large for flue.

The flue area should never be less than $^{1}/_{12}$ the area of the fireplace opening. If this condition exists, reduce the size of the fireplace opening by installing a shallow hood of metal beneath the fireplace breast, raise the hearth or narrow the sides of the opening.

11.   Damper installed too low.

Since the damper is installed within the fireplace, it is unlikely that it can be moved without major work. An alternate solution is to lower the top of the fireplace opening by adding a course or two of brick resting on an angle lintel.

12. Lack of combustion air.

When the house is so weatherproof that the only source of outside air is through the chimney, the fireplace will probably not function properly when the fire is lit. This is due to other appliances, such as stoves and heaters, that require air as part of their operating formula. These appliances draw air that is coming down the fireplace chimney.

There are two ways to solve this problem. Outside air inlets into the firebox will not only solve the problem, but will also make a more energy efficient fireplace. An easier solution is to open a window slightly, so that the air has a means, other than the chimney and fireplace, to enter the house.

13. Chimney flues leak.

Flues subject to deterioration, or those constructed poorly, can leak. This condition is similar to smoking a cigarette with a hole in it. There is no way that the chimney can function properly. The solution is to point the joints in the flue.

A weighted canvas bag stuffed with papers or rags can be lowered in the flue from the top of the chimney. When this plug is just below the flue joint, pour a small amount of grout in the chimney and swab the plug back and forth a few times to finish the joint. Extreme care must be taken not to pour too much grout down the chimney, as it may bypass the plug and land on the smoke shelf, or drain into the fireplace, resulting in damage.

14. Flue off center—Smoke chamber not symmetrical.

If this condition exists, due solely to improper design, the smoke chamber must be rebuilt and the flues realigned.

15.   Inadequate chimney draft.
Two causes of inadequate chimney draft are: insufficient cross-sectional area in the chimney to conduct outdoor, all gases from connecting appliances; and adverse wind pressure patterns at the chimney outlet caused by surrounding structures.

One solution would be added chimney height which would increase the draft and raise the outlet above the turbulence. A second alternative would be to add a draft fan or blower to the venting system to supplement the natural chimney draft and permit an existing chimney to vent the flue gases adequately and safely.

16.   Corrosion of mortar and brick or metal flue.
During combustion, sulfur in the fuel will be converted to sulphur dioxide or to sulphur trioxide, and hydrogen in the fuel will form water vapor. These gases will condense on cold walls of the chimney flue and react to form acids. Such acid formation will occur in any chimney until the liner has been heated enough by the vent gases that its surface temperature is higher than the condensation temperature of the gases.

A chimney liner must resist the corrosive action of these acids. Usually acid corrosion occurs near the top of a chimney where its operating temperature may be so low that condensation can occur.

Factory-built chimneys are designed so that any liquid running down the inside is conducted past the joint between sections and is not scooped into the joint. If the sections are installed upside-down, as may happen when a base section is not used and there is no other indication of which end should be up, acid will accumulate in the joints and will hasten corrosion.

Mortar used to ensure tight joints between the tile liners of masonry chimneys should be a portland cement/sand mix to resist acid attack. Ordinary mortar contains lime which is particularly susceptible to acid attack, and its use for joints between tile liners may lead to premature joint failure. This would permit air to infiltrate into the flue passage to cool the gases and increase condensation in the flue. Acids could also leak through the joint to the outside surface of the liner and attack the mortar of the masonry casing resulting in structural failure of the chimney.

Condensation increases with lower flue gas temperatures. A chimney exposed for its full height to the outdoors will lose more heat, have lower vent gas temperatures and consequently more condensation than the same chimney located inside, therefore an exterior chimney would be expected to deteriorate sooner.

Fireplace and mantel

SECTION 7

STRUCTURAL DESIGN AND SPECIFICATIONS

7.1.   Specifications

Scope: The following specifications, including special items and modifications, shall govern the construction of the fireplace and chimney.

Work Not Included: Any concrete work, furnishing the required vertical reinforcing steel, furnishing or placing vertical steel dowels in the footing.

Work Included: All labor, materials, equipment, appliances, anchors, bolts, miscellaneous iron work and all other reinforcing steel, including setting of vertical steel as indicated on the plans and as herein specified.

Materials: Materials shall be as follows:

> **Water** shall be clean and potable.
> **Sand** conforming to *"Aggregate for Masonry Mortar"*, ASTM C-144.
> **Portland cement** conforming to ASTM C-150.

Hydrated lime conforming to *"Hydrated Lime for Masonry Purposes"*, ASTM C-207, Type S.

Steel reinforcing conforming to *Deformed Billet Steel Bars for Concrete Reinforcement* ASTM A-615--Grade 40 or 60.

Brick meeting the requirements for *"Building Brick"*, ASTM C-62 or ASTM C-216 Face Brick, Grade MW or SW.

Block meeting the requirements for *"Hollow Load Bearing Concrete Masonry Units"*, ASTM C-90, Grade N.

Flue lining conforming to *Clay Flue Linings*, ASTM C-315 or Concrete Flue Liners conforming to ICBO R.R. No. 2602 or Los Angeles City R.R. No. 23878.

Mortar: Mortar shall be composed of one part portland cement and 4 ½ parts dry loose sand to which shall be added not less than ¼ part nor more than ½ hydrated lime, **or** one part portland cement, one part hydrated lime and six parts sand, **or** composed of one part plastic cement and three parts dry loose sand to which lime may be added not in excess of $^1/_{10}$ the volume of cement. All parts by reasonable accurate volume measurements.

Grout: Grout may be composed of mortar retempered with water. Grout must be poured in a fluid state, eight to ten inch (200 mm to 250 mm) slump.

Flue lining shall be held in place with grout. Grout for all fireplaces and for unlined chimneys may consist of retempered mortar slushed into voids.

Mixing of Mortar: All cementitious materials and aggregates shall be mixed for a minimum period of three minutes with the amount of water required to produce the desired workability.

Re-Tempering: Permitted only by adding water within a basin formed of mortar and the mortar reworked into the water.

Mortar which has become harsh and non-plastic shall not be re-tempered or used.

Construction: When the bricks are being laid, they shall be sufficiently damp, and the mortar sufficiently soft, so that the mortar will remain plastic to permit the units to be leveled and plumbed immediately after being laid without losing bond.

All masonry work shall be accurately executed and in conformity with the plans. No brick less than ½ length shall be used in exposed work. Head and bed joints shall be solidly filled with mortar and bricks shall be shoved into place.

In masonry chimney work, tempered mortar grout shall fill the void between the flue lining and the masonry wall.

In fireplace construction do not grout solidly behind the firebox wall. Slush loosely behind the firebox wall to allow for expansion of the firebox.

All joints exposed to the weather shall be tooled.

7.2   *Special Structural Design Consideration*

The structural design, details and clearances shall be in accordance with Sections 3102.3, 3102.4 and 3102.7 of the 1994 Uniform Building Code.

Fireplaces of unusual shapes or size and chimneys of excessive size or height may require special analysis and design to insure proper function and structural stability.

Procedure:

1. Compute size of the flue based on area of fireplace opening.

2. Design smoke shelf and select damper to fit throat.

3. Lay out fireplace, firebox, throat, smoke chamber and chimney.

4. Design chimney for lateral force due to wind or earthquake and provide adequate reinforcing steel. Show ties.

5. If needed, design excessive width for wind or earthquake. Provide adequate reinforcing steel.

6. Design anchorage:

   a. standard anchorage to structure.

   b. special anchorage to structure.

   c. Consider that there is a continuous load path of forces due to wind or earthquake on the chimney to the diaphragm and into the shear walls and into the foundation.

   d. provisions to be made if top plate is interrupted by chimney.

   e. possible evaluation of fireplace and chimney being free standing and independent of structure.

7. Design foundation.

7.3 Structural Design of Chimneys for Earthquake Forces

7.3.1 General

Chimneys are a projecting cantilever element above the roof and are subjected to lateral earthquake forces when the ground shakes.

The 1994 Uniform Building Code Section 3102.4.3, Reinforcing and Seismic Anchorage, prescribes reinforcing and anchorage requirements. The following calculations could be an example for small chimneys and straight up chimneys with either short or extended stacks.

The examples are for Seismic Zone 4, the most severe earthquake exposure condition. For Seismic Zones 3, 2B, 2A and 1, the Z factors would be 0.3, 0.2, 0.15 and 0.075, respectively. Because of the dead weight of the chimney, wind forces generally would not be a governing condition in Seismic Zones 4, 3 and 2B.

7.3.2 Engineering Seismic Factors

The lateral seismic force is based on the formula:

$$F_P = Z I C_p W_P$$

From 1994 UBC Table 16-0 —Horizontal Force Factor, C_p

2. Nonstructural components

    2. Chimney, stacks, trussed towers and tanks on legs:
       a. Supported on or projecting as an unbraced cantilever above the roof more than one half their total height 2.00

> b.   All others, including those supported below the roof with unbraced projection above the roof less than one half its height 0.75

The distance from the top of the fireplace foundation to the top of the chimney is considered the total height of the chimney for the determination of C_p. The chimney above the roof tie should be one half or less the total height. Therefore $C_p = 0.75$ for the majority of chimneys.

Seismic Zone 4; $Z = 0.4$
Importance factor; $I = 1.0$
Horizontal force factor $C_p = 0.75$
Weight of part; W_p

$F_P = 0.4 \times 1.0 \times 0.75\ W_p$
$\quad = 0.3\ W_p$

Chimney under engineering calculations

7.3.3   Small Chimney, 4 ft. above Roof Tie

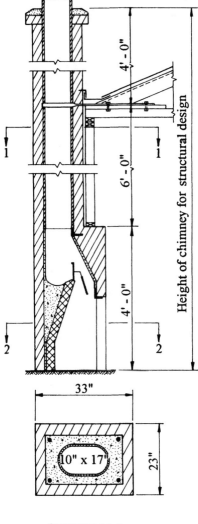

SECTION 1-1

Figure 7-1A   Small chimney above fire box, 4 feet above roof tie

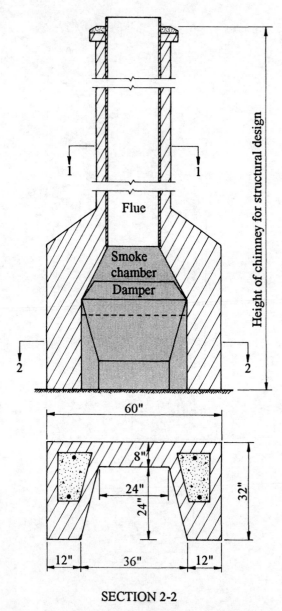

SECTION 2-2

Figure 7-1B Small chimney above fire box, 4 feet above roof tie

Weight of chimney - (Cross-section - flue area)

$$W_p = \left(\frac{23 \times 33}{144} - 0.8 \right) 120 = 536 \text{ lbs / ft}$$

Reinforcing 4 #4 bars, 1 each corner $d = 23" - 5" = 18"$

Steel ratio $p = \dfrac{A_s}{bd} = \dfrac{2 \times 0.20}{33 \times 18} = 0.00067$

Seismic lateral force, F_p
$$F_P = Z \, I \, C_P \, W_P = 0.4 \times 1 \times 0.75 \times 536$$
$$= 160 \text{ lbs/ft}$$

Chimney extends 4 ft. above tie, moment at roof tie
$$M = wh^2/2 = 160 \times 4^2/2 = 1280 \text{ ft.lbs}$$

Flexural coefficient at roof tie due to moment

$$1.33K = \frac{M}{bd^2}$$
$$= \frac{1280 \times 12}{33 \times 18^2} = 1.4$$

From Table E1a Reinforced Masonry Engineering Handbook, 5th Edition, Updated, (page 326) for $1.33K = 1.4$ read $p = 0.0002$

Reinforcing specified is in excess of requirement.

Check shear at roof tie, height = 4 ft.

Lateral seismic force = 4 x 160 = 640 lbs.

Shear stress $v = \dfrac{V}{bjd} = \dfrac{640}{33 \times .9 \times 18} = 1.2 \text{ psi}$ O.K.

Assume masonry on sides of chimney only, parallel to force.

Shear stress $v = \dfrac{640}{2 \times 4 \times 18} = 4.4$ psi   O.K.

Anchor tie to roof or diaphragm, 4 ft. below top of chimney.

Assume cantilever chimney plus ½ height above fire box and below tie contributing lateral load to roof tie.

Lateral load $= \left(4 + \dfrac{6}{2}\right)160 = 1120$ lbs

Use 2 anchor ties, $^3/_{16}$" x 1", tie hook to engage rear reinforcing bar.

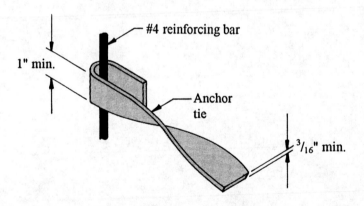

1" min.

— #4 reinforcing bar

— Anchor tie

$^3/_{16}$" min.

Load/tie = 1120 ÷ 2 = 560 lbs

Secure tie to 2" x 4" runner or joists with 2 - ½" dia. bolts 2" long or 2-$^3/_8$" dia. lag screws 3" long.

Allowable single shear on ½ bolts - Douglas fir(s) G = 0.46; with side plate $Z_{\parallel} = 500$ lbs, $Z_{\perp} = 250$ lbs. (UBC Table 23-III-K Page 2-1004).

Allowable single shear on $^3/_8$" dia. lag screws, Douglas fir(s) G = 0.46; with side plate $Z_{\parallel}$ = 390 lbs; $Z_{\perp}$ = 220 lbs. (UBC Table 23-III-U Page 2-1029).

Secure 2" x 4" to joists or rafters with 8-16d common nails @ 131 lbs/nail x 1.33 = 174 lbs; UBC Table 23-III-II, Page 2-1061.

Use 2-16d common nails into each joist or rafter and cross 4 members, total 8 nails.
8 x 174 = 1,394# / tie > 560# required.

7.3.4   Small Chimney, 10 ft. above Roof Tie

From top of foundation to top of chimney = 20 ft., total height

Reinforcing A_s = 2 #4 bars each side

Steel ratio $p = \dfrac{2 \times 0.2}{33 \times 18} = 0.00067$

From Table E1a of Reinforced Masonry Engineering Handbook, 5th Edition, Updated, (page 326) for $p = 0.00067$.

read $1.33K = 17.5 = \dfrac{M}{bd^2}$

$$M = 17.5 \, bd^2 = 17.5 \, (33 \times 18^2)/12$$
$$= 15,590 \text{ ft.lbs}$$

Maximum height of cantilevered chimney based on moment capacity.

$$M = wh^2/2 \qquad h = \sqrt{\dfrac{2M}{w}}$$

$$h = \sqrt{\frac{2 \times 15590}{160}} = 14 \text{ ft. maximum; use 10 ft. O.K.}$$

Lateral seismic force = 10 x 160 = 1600 lbs

$$\text{Shear stress } v = \frac{V}{bjd} = \frac{1600}{33 \times .9 \times 18} = 3 \text{ psi} \quad \text{O.K.}$$

Assume masonry only parallel to force.

$$\text{Shear stress} \quad v = \frac{1600}{2 \times 4 \times 18} = 11 \text{ psi} \ < 20 \text{ psi O.K.}$$

Anchorage load from chimney to diaphragm.

Assume cantilever chimney plus one half of height above firebox and below tie contributing to lateral load to roof tie.

$$\text{Lateral load} = \left(10 + \frac{6}{2}\right)160 = 2080 \text{ lbs}$$

Load/tie = 2080/2 = 1040 lbs/tie

Secure tie to 2" x 4" runner that crosses at least 4 joists or directly to joists with four ½" dia. bolts 2" long (UBC Table 23-III-K) or 4-$^3/_8$" dia. lag screws 3" long (UBC Table 23-III-U) thru 2" x 4" and into joists - Provide blocking between joists and under 2" x 4".

Allow shear load = 220x 1.33 x 4 = 1173 lbs > 1040 lbs O.K.

Secure 2" x 4" runner to 4 joists or rafters with 16d common nails @ 131 lbs x 1.33 = 174 lbs/nail (UBC Table 23-III-II).

$$\text{No. of nails} = \frac{1147}{174} = 7 \text{ nails(use 2 nails/joist)}$$

Check shear through chimney $V = 2080$ lbs

Shear stress $\quad v = \dfrac{V}{bjd} = \dfrac{2080}{33 \text{ x } .9 \text{ x } 18} = 3.9$ psi   O.K.

Assume only masonry on side, parallel to lateral force.

Shear stress $\quad v = \dfrac{2080}{2 \text{ x } 4 \text{ x } 18} = 14$ psi < 20 psi O.K.

NOTE: The flexural stress and shear stress through the firebox will not exceed those in the chimney.

   Chimneys must be anchored to the roof or floor diaphragm in order to stabilize it against seismic forces.   Much consideration is given as to whether the house holds up the chimney or the chimney holds up the house.   The K & W Mfg. Co. Inc. of Corona, California, has developed a special earthquake chimney anchor that can resist lateral forces to a prescribed level and then deforms to absorb excess energy.

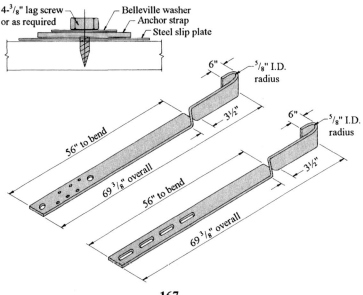

7.3.5 *Straight up Chimney the Same Width as the Fire Box*

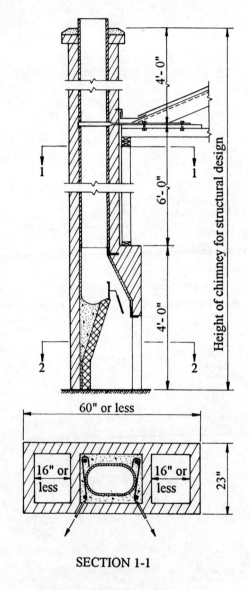

SECTION 1-1

Figure 7-2A Straight up chimney

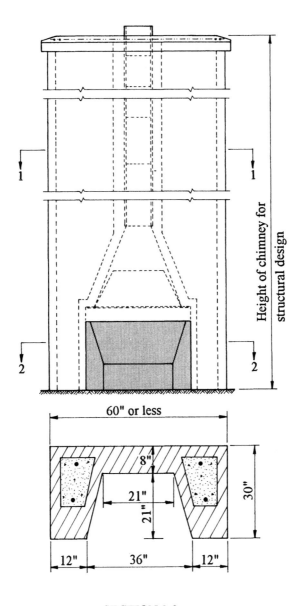

SECTION 2-2

Figure 7-2B   Straight up chimney

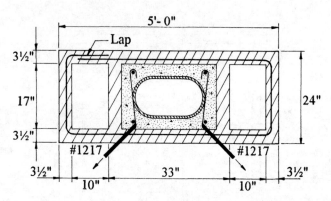

Weight of chimney $= \left(2 \times 5 - \dfrac{2 \times 10 \times 17}{144} - 0.8 \right) 120 = 820$ lbs/ft.

Reinforcing 6 #4 bars, 3 each side, $d = 24 - (3\frac{1}{2}" + 1\frac{1}{2}") = 19"$

Steel ratio $p = \dfrac{A_s}{bd} = \dfrac{3 \times 0.2}{60 \times 19} = 0.00053$

Seismic lateral force $F_P = Z \, I \, C_P \, W_P = 0.4 \times 1 \times 0.75 \times 820$
$= 246$ lbs/ft.

Chimney extends 4 ft. above roof tie, moment at roof tie.

$$M = wh^2/2 = 246 \times 4^2/2 = 1968 \text{ ft.lbs/ft.}$$

Flexural coefficient at roof tie due to moment.

$$1.33K = \dfrac{M}{bd^2} = \dfrac{1968 \times 12}{60 \times 19^2} = 1.1$$

From Table E1a Reinforced Masonry Engineering Handbook, 5th Edition, Updated, (page 326) for $1.33K = 1.1$ read $p = 0.0002$

Reinforcing specified is in excess of requirements.

Check shear at roof tie, height = 4 ft.

Lateral seismic force = 4 x 246 = 984 lbs

Shear stress $\quad v = \dfrac{V}{bjd} = \dfrac{984}{60 \text{ x } .9 \text{ x } 19} = 1$ psi   O.K.

Assume masonry on side of chimney only parallel to force.

Shear stress $\quad v = \dfrac{984}{2 \text{ x } 4 \text{ x } 19} = 6.5$ psi   O.K.

Anchor tie at roof or diaphragm for chimney height of 4 ft.

Assume cantilever chimney plus ½ height above firebox and below tie contributing to lateral load to roof tie.

Lateral load = $\left(4 + \dfrac{6}{2} \right)$ 246 = 1722 lbs

Provide 2 anchor ties.

Load/tie = $\dfrac{1722}{2} = 861$ lbs (direct load)

Load @ 45° = $\sqrt{2}$ x 861 = 1217 lbs

$^3/_8$" dia. lag screws @ 390 lbs/lag screws

use 3 lag screws 2" long
3 x 390 x 1.33 = 1561 lbs > 1217 lbs O.K.

Secure 2" x 4" runner to 4 joists or rafters with 16d common nails, @ 131 lbs/nail x 1.33 = 174 lbs/nail.
No. of nails = $\dfrac{1217}{174} = 7$ nails (use 8 nails)

Use 2 nails per joist or rafter crossing 4 members with runner for a total of 8 nails.

7.3.6   *Straight up Chimney for 10 ft. above Tie*

From top of foundation to top of chimney = 20 ft.; total height.

Reinforcing A_s = three #4 bars each side.

Steel ratio $p = \dfrac{A_s}{bd} = \dfrac{3 \times 0.2}{60 \times 19} = 0.00053$

From Table E1a of Reinforced Masonry Engineering Handbook, 5th Edition, Updated, (page 326) for $p = 0.00053$.

read $1.33K = 15.4 = \dfrac{M}{bd^2}$

$$M = 15.4 \, bd^2/12$$
$$= 15.4 \times 60 \times 19^2/12 = 27,800 \text{ ft lbs}$$

Maximum height of cantilevered chimney based on moment capacity.

$$M = wh^2/2$$

$$h = \sqrt{\frac{2M}{w}} = \sqrt{\frac{2 \times 27800}{267}}$$

$$= 14.4 \text{ ft say 14 ft. Use 10 ft.}$$

Lateral seismic force = 10 x 246 = 2460 lbs

Shear stress $v = \dfrac{V}{bjd} = \dfrac{2460}{60 \times .9 \times 19} = 2.4 \text{psi}$ O.K.

Anchor load from chimney to diaphragm.

Assume cantilever chimney plus one half of height above firebox and of chimney below tie contributing to lateral load of roof tie.

Lateral load $= \left(10 + \dfrac{6}{2}\right) 246 = 3198$ lbs

Load/tie $= 3470/2 = 1735$ lbs

Load at $45° = \sqrt{2 \times 1735} = 2454$ lbs

Secure tie to 2" x 4" runner that crosses at least 4 joists or directly to joists.

½" dia. bolts allowable $500 \times 1.33 = 667$ lbs each

No. of bolts $= \dfrac{2454}{667} = 4$ bolts/ties

Secure tie to 2" x 4" runner or to joists with 16d common nails.

$= 131 \times 1.33 = 174$ lbs

No. of nails $= \dfrac{2454}{174} = 15$ nails; 3 nails/joist; nail to 5 joists

Check shear through chimney.

Lateral shear load $= 2460$ lbs

Shear stress $\quad v = \dfrac{V}{bjd} = \dfrac{2460}{60 \times .9 \times 19} = 2.4 \, \text{psi}$ O.K.

NOTE: If a high chimney is required or desired, proper anchorage to the structure is vital for structural safety. Detailed analysis by a qualified engineer is necessary.

By use of a chimney top an additional two feet of height can be readily obtained with only a small increase in weight and lateral forces. See Section 5.18.1 Chimney Tops or Pots.

7.4   *Veneer on Chimney and Fireplace*

Many chimneys and fireplaces are built with common brick or block and are given a special architectural appearance with a veneer stone, marble or other selected material. The application of this veneer material to the fireplace or chimney should follow code requirements as outlined in the applicable building code and as explained in the Masonry Institute of America publication *"Masonry Veneer"*.

Chimney veneered with stone

CODE REQUIREMENTS

8.1   General

In general, the requirements, details and specifications for fireplaces and chimneys are set forth in local building codes. Table 8-B is a compilation of the requirements for the Uniform Building Code, and the FHA and VA.

These requirements are keyed to the cross-sectional drawings of the chimneys, both unlined and lined. These code requirements are for a single residential fireplace with the chimney tied to the roof or ceiling rafters.

In the event the chimney is multi-story, extra wide or extra high, or there are multiple fireplaces and flues within the chimney, special consideration in design should be provided.

8.2   *Brick Fireplace and Chimney*

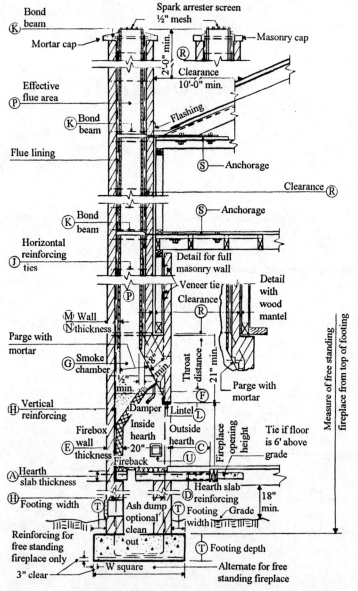

Figure 8-1   Brick firebox and chimney with wood floors

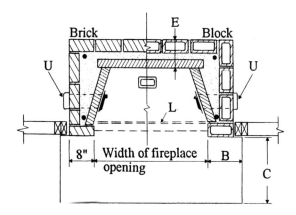

Figure 8-2   Plan at top of hearth

8.3   *Brick Corner Fireplace*

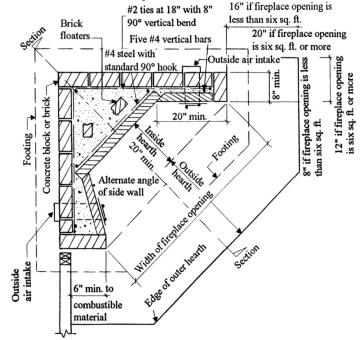

Figure 8-3   Plan at top of hearth for corner fireplace

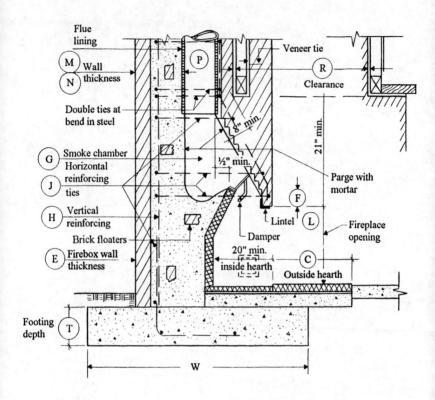

Figure 8-4 **Cross-section through firebox of a corner fireplace**

Corner fireplace

8.4   Block Fireplace and Chimney   4 inch (102 mm) wide units

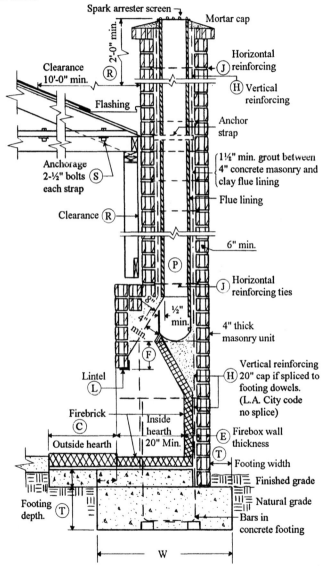

Figure 8-5   4 inch (102 mm) block firebox and chimney on concrete slab

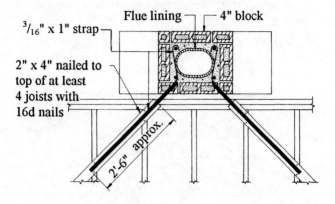

Figure 8-6 Chimney and anchorage plan—4 inch (102 mm) CMU

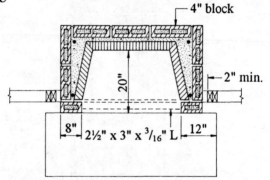

Figure 8-7 Fireplace plan—4 inch (102 mm) CMU

Table 8-A Equivalent Solid Thickness*

Nominal Thickness		Equivalent Solid Thickness	
Hollow Masonry Units			
Inches	mm	Inches	mm
4	102	2.2	56
6	152	3.4	86
8	203	4.0	102
*Cells without reinforcing steel not grouted			

Table 8-B General Code Requirements

ITEM	Letter	Uniform Building Code	FHA & VA
Hearth Slab Thickness	A	4"	4"
Hearth Slab Width (Each side of opening)	B	8" if Fireplace opening < 6 sq.ft. 12" if fireplace opening ≥ 6 sq.ft.	8"
Hearth Slab Length (Each side of opening)	C	18"	16"
Hearth Slab Reinforcing	D	Reinforced to carry its own weight and all imposed loads	Required if cantilevered in connection with raised wood floor construction
Thickness of Wall of Firebox	E	10" common brick or 8" where a firebrick lining is used	8" including minimum 2" firebrick lining—12" when no lining is provided
Distance from Top of Opening to Throat	F	6"	6" min.; 8" recommended
Smoke Chamber Edge of Shelf	G		½" offset
Rear wall thickness Rear Wall-Thickness Front & Side Wall Thickness		6" 8"	6" plus parging; may be omitted if wall thickness is 8" or more of solid masonry. Form damper is required
Chimney Vertical Reinforcing	H	Four #4 full length bars for chimney up to 40" wide. Add two #4 bars for each additional 40" of width	Four #4 bars full length, no splice unless welded
Horizontal Reinforcing	J	¼" ties @ 18" and 2 ties at each bent in vertical steel	¼" bars at 24"
Bond Beams	K	No special requirements	Two ¼" bars at top bond beam 4" high Two ¼" bars at anchorage bond beam 5" high

Note: For metric dimensions in millimeters multiply by 25.4

Table 8-B General Code Requirements - Continued

ITEM	Letter	Uniform Building Code	FHA & VA
Fireplace Lintel	L	noncombustible	2½" x 3" x ³/₁₆" angle with 3" end bearing
Chimney Walls with Flue Lining	M	Brick with grout around lining, 4" min. from flue lining to outside face of chimney	Brick with grout around lining, 4" min. from outside flue lining to outside face of chimney
Chimney Walls with Unlined Flue	N	8" Solid masonry	8" Solid masonry
Distance Between Adjacent Flues	O	4" including flue liner	4" wythe for brick
Effective Flue Area (Based on Area of Fireplace Opening)	P	Round lining - 1/12, 50 sq.in. min. Rectangular lining 1/10 or 65 sq.in. min. Unlined or lined with firebrick - 1/8, 100 sq.in. min.	1/10 for chimneys over 15' high and over 1/8 for chimneys less than 15' high
Clearances Wood Frame Combustible Material	R	1" when outside of wall or ½" gypsum board 2" when entirely within structure 6" min. to fireplace opening 12" from opening when material projects more than 1/8" for each 1" from opening 2' above highest point within 10' of chimney	¾" from subfloor or floor or roof sheathing 2" from framing members 3½" to edge of fireplace 12" from opening when projecting more than 1½"
Chimney Above Roof			2' above highest point within 10' of chimney

Note: For metric dimensions in millimeters multiply by 25.4

Table 8-B General Code Requirements - Continued

ITEM	Letter	Uniform Building Code	FHA & VA
Anchorage Strap Number Embedment into chimney Fasten to Bolts Laps Nails	S	3/16" x 1" 2 12" hooked around outer bar with 6" ext. 4 joists two ½" diameter Six - 16d	1/4" x 1" 2 18" hooked around outer bar 3 joists two ½" diameter Six - 16d
Footing Thickness Width	T	12" min. 6" each side of fireplace wall	8" min. for 1 story chimney 12" min. for 2 story chimney 6" each side of fireplace wall
Outside Air Intakes	U	Optional	6 sq. in, min. area (California Energy Requirement)
Glass Screen Door		Optional	Required, but shall not interfere with energy conservation requirements

Note: For metric dimensions in millimeters multiply by 25.4

Table 8-C Foundation Requirements for One-Story free Standing Fireplace; Soil Bearing 1000 pf (47.9 kPa) min.

Free standing height		Square footing "W" (min.)		Bottom reinf. each way	Free standing height		Square footing "W" (min.)		Bottom reinf. each way
Ft.	(m)	Ft.	(m)		Ft.	(m)	Ft.	(m)	
10 and 11	3.0-3.4	4'-0"	1.2	4 #4	14 and 15	4.3-4.6	5'-0"	1.5	5 #4
12 and 13	3.7-4.0	4'-6"	1.4	4 #4	16 and 17	4.9-5.2	5'-6"	1.7	5 #4

8.5 Block Fireplace and Chimney, 6 inch (152 mm) and 8 inch (203 mm) Wide Units

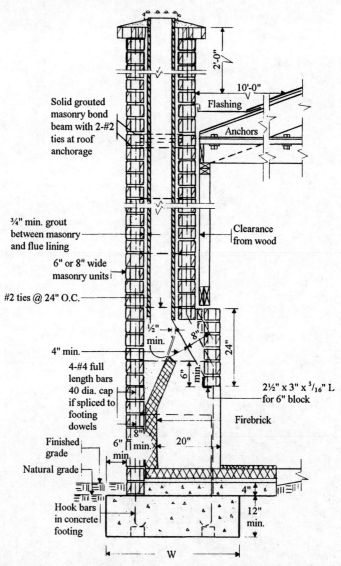

Figure 8-8 6 inch (152 mm) and 8 inch (203 mm) Block fireplace and chimney

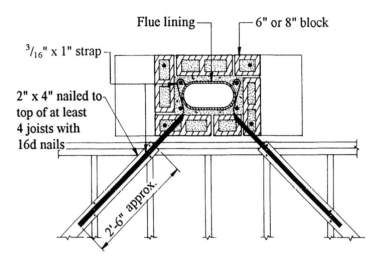

Figure 8-9   Chimney and anchorage plan. 6 inch (152 mm) and 8 inch (203 mm) block

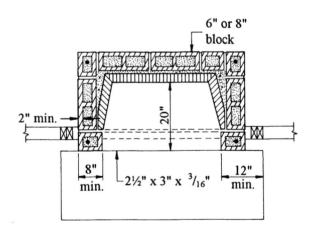

Figure 8-10   Fireplace plan. 6 inch (152 mm) and 8 inch (203 mm) block

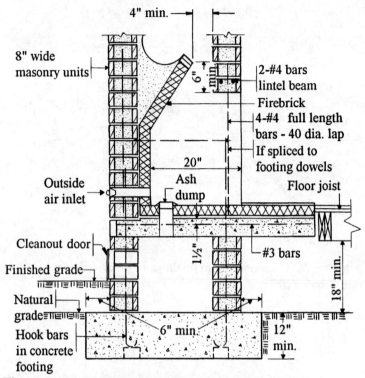

8" wide masonry units

4" min.

6" min.

2-#4 bars lintel beam

Firebrick

4-#4 full length bars - 40 dia. lap

If spliced to footing dowels

20"

Ash dump

Floor joist

Outside air inlet

Cleanout door

1½"

#3 bars

18" min.

Finished grade

Natural grade

Hook bars in concrete footing

6" min.

12" min.

Figure 8-11   Vertical section - 8 inch (203 mm) block (wood floor)

Concrete flue liners to be installed in chimney

CODE EXCERPTS

9.1   Uniform Building Code, 1994 Edition

Chapter 31 of the Uniform Building Code, 1994 edition, copyright © 1994, Section 3102, Chimneys, Fireplaces and Barbecues, and the 1994 Analysis of Revision of Chapter 31 of the Uniform Building Code, copyright © 1994, have been reproduced with permission of the publishers, the International Conference of Building Officials, 5360 South Workman Mill Road, Whittier, California 90601

Uniform Building Code, 1994 Edition

CHAPTER 31

SECTION 3102 -- CHIMNEYS, FIREPLACES AND BARBECUES

3102.1 Scope. Chimneys, flues, fireplaces and barbecues, and their connections, carrying products of combustion shall conform to the requirements of this section.

3102.2 Definitions.

BARBECUES is a stationary open hearth or brazier, either fuel fired or electric, used for food preparation.

CHIMNEY is a hollow shaft containing one or more passageways, vertical or nearly so, for conveying products of combustion to the outside atmosphere.

CHIMNEY CLASSIFICATIONS:

Chimney, High-heat Industrial Appliance-type, is a factory built, masonry or metal chimney suitable for removing the products of combustion from fuel-burning high-heat appliances producing combustion gases in excess of 2,000°F. (1093°C.) measured at the appliance flue outlet.

Chimney, Low-heat Industrial Appliance-type, is a factory built, masonry or metal chimney suitable for removing the products of combustion from fuel-burning low-heat appliances producing combustion gases not in excess of 1,000°F.(538°C.) under normal operating conditions but capable of producing combustion gases of 1,400°F.(760°C.) during intermittent forced firing for periods up to one hour. All temperatures are measured at the appliance flue outlet.

Chimney, Medium-heat Industrial Appliance-type, is a factory built, masonry or metal chimney suitable for removing the products of combustion from fuel-burning medium-heat appliances producing combustion gases not in excess of 2,000° F.(1093°C.) measured at the appliance flue outlet.

Chimney, Residential Appliance-type, is a factory-built or masonry chimney suitable for removing products of combustion from residential-type appliances producing combustion gases not in excess of 1000°F.(538°C.) measured at the appliance flue outlet.

CHIMNEY CONNECTOR is the pipe or breeching which connects a fuel-burning appliance to a chimney (See Chapter 9, Mechanical Code).

CHIMNEY, FACTORY-BUILT, is a chimney manufactured at a location other than the building site and composed of listed factory-built components assembled in accordance with the terms of the listing to form the completed chimney.

CHIMNEY LINER is a lining material of fireclay or approved fireclay refractory brick. For guideline standard on fireclay refractory brick see Section 3502 and 3503, ASTM C 27, Fireclay Refractories.

FIREBRICK is a refractory brick

FIREPLACE is a hearth and fire chamber or similar prepared place in which a fire may be made and which is built in conjunction with a chimney.

FACTORY-BUILT FIREPLACE is a listed assembly of a fire chamber, its chimney and related factory-made parts designed for unit assembly without requiring field construction. Factory-built fireplaces are not dependent upon mortar-filled joints for continued safe use.

MASONRY FIREPLACE is a hearth and fire chamber of solid masonry units such as bricks, stones, masonry units, or reinforced concrete provided with a suitable chimney.

MASONRY CHIMNEY is a chimney of masonry units, bricks, stones or listed masonry chimney units lined with approved flue liners. For the purpose of this chapter, masonry chimneys shall include reinforced concrete chimneys.

3102.3 Chimneys, General

3102.3.1 Chimney Support. Chimneys shall be designed, anchored, supported and reinforced as required in this chapter and applicable provisions of Chapters 16, 18, 19, 21 and 22 of this code. A chimney shall not support any structural load other than its own weight unless designed as a supporting member.

3102.3.2 Construction. Each chimney shall be so constructed as to safely convey flue gases not exceeding the maximum temperatures for the type of construction as set forth in Table No. 31-B and shall be capable of producing a draft at the appliance not less than that required for safe operation.

3102.3.3 Clearance. Clearance to combustible material shall be as required by Table No. 31-B.

3102.3.4 Lining. When required by Table No. 31-B, chimneys shall be lined with fireclay flue tile, firebrick, molded refractory units or other approved lining not less than $^5/_8$ inch (15.9 mm) thick as set forth in Table No. 31-B. Chimney liners shall be carefully bedded in approved mortar with close-fitting joints left smooth on the inside.

3102.3.5 Area. Chimney passageways shall be not smaller in area than the vent connection on the appliance attached thereto nor less than that set forth in Table No. 31-A, unless engineering methods approved by the building official have been used to design the system.

3102.3.6 Height and Termination. Every chimney shall extend above the roof and the highest elevation of any part of a building as shown in Table No. 31-B. For altitudes over 2,000 feet (610 m), the building official shall be consulted in determining the height of the chimney.

3102.3.7 Cleanouts. Cleanout openings shall be provided within 6 inches (152 mm) of the base of every masonry chimney.

3102.3.8 Spark Arrester. Where determined necessary by the building official due to local climatic conditions or where sparks escaping from the chimney would create a hazard, chimneys attached to any appliance or fireplace that burns solid fuel shall be equipped with an approved spark arrester. The net free area of the spark arrester shall not be less than four times the net free area of the outlet of the chimney. The spark arrester screen shall have heat and corrosion resistance equivalent to 0.109 inch (2.77 mm) (No. 12 B.W. gage) wire, 0.047 inch (1.07 mm) (No. 19 B.W. gage) galvanized wire or 0.022 inch (0.56 mm) (No. 24 B.W. gage) stainless steel. Openings shall not permit the passage of spheres having a diameter larger than ½ inch (12.7 mm) and shall not block the passage of spheres having a diameter of least than $^3/_8$ inch (9.5 mm).

Chimneys used with fireplaces or heating appliances in which solid or liquid fuel is used shall be provided with a spark arrester as required in the Fire Code.

> **EXCEPTION:** *Chimneys which are located more than 200 feet (60 960 mm) from any mountainous, brush-covered or forest-covered land or land covered with flammable material and are not attached to a structure having less than a Class C roof covering, as set forth in Chapter 15.*

3102.4 Masonry Chimneys.

3102.4.1 Design. Masonry chimneys shall be designed and constructed to comply with Sections 3102.3.2 and 3102.4.2.

3102.4.2. Walls. Walls of masonry chimneys shall be constructed as set forth in Table No. 31-B.

3102.4.3 Reinforcing and seismic anchorage. Unless a specific design is provided, every masonry or concrete chimney in Seismic Zones No. 2, 3 and 4 shall be reinforced with not less than four No. 4 steel reinforcing bars conforming to the provisions of Chapter 19 or 21 of this code. The bars shall extend the full height of the chimney and shall be spliced in accordance with the applicable requirements of Chapter 19 or 21. In masonry chimneys the vertical bars shall have a minimum cover of ½ inch (13 mm) of grout or mortar tempered to a pouring consistency. The bars shall be tied horizontally at 18-inch (457 mm) intervals with not less than ¼-inch (6.4 mm)-diameter steel ties. The slope of the inclined portion of the offset in vertical bars shall not exceed 2 units vertical in 1 horizontal (200% slope). Two ties shall also be placed at each bend in vertical bars. Where the width of the chimney exceeds 40 inches (1016 mm), two additional No. 4 vertical bars shall be provided for each additional flue incorporated in the chimney or for each additional 40 inches (1016 mm) in width or fraction thereof.

In Seismic Zones No. 2, 3 and 4, all masonry and concrete chimneys shall be anchored at each floor or ceiling line more than 6 feet (1829 mm) above grade, except when constructed completely within the exterior walls of the building. Anchorage shall consist of two $^3/_{16}$-inch by 1-inch (4.8 mm by 25 mm) steel straps cast at least 12 inches (305 mm) into the chimney with a 180-degree bend with a 6-inch (152 mm) extension around the vertical reinforcing bars in the outer face of the chimney.

Each strap shall be fastened to the structural framework of the building with two ½-inch-diameter (12.7 mm) bolts per strap. Where the joists do not head into the chimney, the anchor straps shall be connected to 2-inch by 4-inch (51 mm by 102 mm) ties crossing a minimum of four joists. The ties shall be connected to each joist with two 16d nails. As an alternative to the 2-inch by 4-inch (51 mm by 102 mm) ties, each anchor strap shall be connected to the structural framework by two ½-inch-diameter (12.7 mm) bolts in an approved manner.

3102.4.4   Chimney Offset. Masonry chimneys may be offset at a slope of not more than 4 inches in 24 inches (102 mm in 610 mm), but not more than one third of the dimension of the chimney, in the direction of the offset. The slope of the transition from the fireplace to the chimney shall not exceed 2 units vertical in 1 unit horizontal (200% slope).

3102.4.5   Change in Size or Shape. Changes in the size or shape of a masonry chimney, where the chimney passes through the roof, shall not be made within a distance of 6 inches (152 mm) above or below the roof joists or rafters.

3102.4.6   Separation of Masonry Chimney Passageways. Two or more flues in a chimney shall be separated by masonry not less than 4 inches (102 mm) thick bonded into the masonry wall of the chimney.

3102.4.7   Inlets. Every inlet to any masonry chimney shall enter the side thereof and shall be of not less than $^1/_8$-inch-thick (3.2 mm) metal or $^5/_8$-inch-thick (16 mm) refractory material. Where there is no other opening below the inlet other than the cleanout, a masonry plug shall be constructed in the chimney not more than 16 inches (406 mm) below the inlet and the cleanout shall be located where it is accessible above the plug. If the plug is located less than 6 inches (152 mm) below the inlet, the inlet may serve as the cleanout.

3102.5   Factory-built Chimneys and Fireplaces.

3102.5.1   General. Factory-built chimneys and factory-built fireplaces shall be listed and shall be installed in accordance with the terms of their listings and the manufacturer's instructions as specified in the Mechanical Code.

3102.5.2 Hearth Extensions. Hearth extensions of listed factory-built fireplaces shall conform to the conditions of listing and the manufacturer's installation instructions.

3102.5.3 Multiple Venting in Vertical Shafts. Factory-built chimneys utilized with listed factory-built fireplaces may be used in a common vertical shaft having the required fire-resistance rating.

3102.6 Metal Chimneys. Metal chimneys shall be constructed and installed to meet the requirements of the Mechanical Code.

Metal chimneys shall be anchored at each floor and roof with two 1½-inch by ⅛-inch (38 mm by 3.2 mm) metal straps looped around the outside of the chimney installation and nailed with not less than six 8d nails per strap at each joist.

3102.7 Masonry and Concrete Fireplace and Barbecues.

Analysis of Section 3102.7 In general, Section 3102.7 was Section 3707 in the 1991 U.B.C. Section 3707 (n) of the 1991 U.B.C. has been deleted to ensure that unvented appliances are not installed in an imitation fireplace. The *Uniform Mechanical Code* now prohibits unvented fuel-fired appliances in any building (see U.M.C. Section 327.6).

3102.7.1. General. Masonry fireplaces, barbecues, smoke chambers and fireplace chimneys shall be of masonry or reinforced concrete and shall conform to the requirements of this section.

3102.7.2 Support. Masonry fireplaces shall be supported on foundations designed as specified in Chapters 16, 18 and 21.

When approved design is not provided, foundations for masonry and concrete fireplaces shall not be less than 12 inches (305 mm) thick, extend not less than 6 inches (152 mm) outside the fireplace wall and project below the natural ground surface in accordance with the depth of foundations set forth in Table 18-1-D.

3102.7.3 Fireplace Wall. Masonry walls of fireplaces shall be not less than 8 inches (203 mm) in thickness. Walls of fireboxes shall be not less than 10 inches (254 mm) in thickness, except that where a lining of firebrick is used, such walls shall be not less than a total of 8 inches (203 mm) in thickness. The firebox shall be not less than 20 inches (508 mm) in depth. Joints in firebrick shall not exceed ¼ inch (6 mm).

EXCEPTION: For Rumford fireplaces, the depth may be reduced to 12 inches (305 mm) when:
1. The depth is at least one third the width of the fireplace opening.
2. The throat is at least 12 inches (305 mm) above the lintel and is at least $1/20$ of the cross-sectional area of the fireplace opening.

Analysis of Exception:

Sec. 3102.7.3   The new exception provides dimensional criteria to permit the installation of Rumford fireplaces. These fireplaces were common in the late 1700s until mid-1800s when coal-and gas-burning fireplaces became popular. The *Uniform Building Code*, however, tended to favor a particular type of fireplace designed in the 1940s which is much deeper and lower than the Rumford fireplace. The existing firebox depth and throat size requirements are intended to ensure that the fireplace draws well, regardless of its efficiency, but these requirements prohibit the construction of a Rumford fireplace. Rumford fireplaces, when built in accordance with the specified limitation, have performed safely.

3102.7.4 Hoods. Metal hoods used as part of a fireplace or barbecue shall be not less than 0.036 inch (0.92 mm) (No 19 carbon sheet steel gage) copper, galvanized steel or other equivalent corrosion-resistant ferrous metal with all seams and connections of smokeproof unsoldered constructions. The hoods shall be sloped at an angle of 45 degrees or less from the vertical and shall extend horizontally at least 6 inches (152 mm) beyond the limits of the firebox. Metal hoods shall be kept a minimum of 18 inches (457 mm) from combustible materials unless approved for reduced clearances.

3102.7.5 Metal Heat Circulators. Approved metal heat circulators may be installed in fireplaces.

3102.7.6 Smoke Chamber. Front and side walls shall be not less than 8 inches (203 mm) in thickness. Smoke chamber back walls shall be not less than 6 inches (152 mm) in thickness.

3102.7.7 Chimneys. Chimneys for fireplaces shall be constructed as specified in Sections 3102.3, 3102.4 and 3102.5 for residential-type appliances.

3102.7.8 Clearance to Combustible Material. Combustible materials shall not be placed within 2 inches (51 mm) of fireplace, smoke chamber or chimney walls. Combustible material shall not be placed within 6 inches (152 mm) of the fireplace opening. No such combustible material within 12 inches (305 mm) of the fireplace opening shall project more than $^1/_8$ inch (3 mm) for each 1-inch (25 mm) clearance from such opening.

No part of metal hoods used as part of a fireplace or barbecue shall be less than 18 inches (457 mm) from combustible material. This clearance may be reduced to the minimum requirements specified in the Mechanical Code.

3102.7.9 Areas of Flues, Throats and Dampers. The net cross-sectional area of the flue and of the throat between the firebox and the smoke chamber of a fireplace shall not be less than as set forth in Table 31-A. Metal dampers equivalent to not less than 0.097 inch (2.46 mm) (No. 12 carbon sheet metal gage steel shall be installed. When fully opened, damper openings shall not be less than 90 percent of the required flue area.

3102.7.10 Lintel. Masonry over the fireplace opening shall be supported by a noncombustible lintel.

3102.7.11 Hearth. Masonry fireplaces shall be provided with a brick, concrete, stone or other approved noncombustible hearth slab. This slab shall not be less than 4 inches (102 mm) thick and shall be supported by noncombustible materials or reinforced to carry its own weight and all imposed loads. Combustible forms and centering shall be removed.

3102.7.12 Hearth extensions. Hearths shall extend at least 16 inches (406 mm) from the front of, and at least 8 inches (203 mm) beyond each side of, the fireplace opening. Where the fireplace opening is 6 square feet (0.56 m^2) or larger, the hearth extension shall extend at least 20 inches (508 mm) in front of, and at least 12 inches (305 mm) beyond each side of, the fireplace opening.

Except for fireplaces which open to the exterior of the building, the hearth slab shall be readily distinguishable from the surrounding or adjacent floor.

3102.7.13 Fire blocking. Fire blocking between chimneys and combustible construction shall meet the requirements specified in Section 708.

Table No. 31-A   Minimum Passageway Areas for Masonry Chimneys[1]

Minimum Cross-sectional Area			
	x 645 for sq. mm.		
	Tile Lined		
Type of Masonry Chimney	Round	Square or Rectangle	Lined with Firebrick or Unlined
1. Residential	50 sq.in.	50 sq. in.	85 sq. in.
2. Fireplace[2]	$1/12$ of opening Minimum 50 sq.in.	$1/10$ of opening Minimum 64 sq.in.	$1/8$ of opening Minimum 100 sq.in.
3. Low heat	50 sq.in.	57 sq.in.	135 sq.in.
4. Incinerator Apartment type 1 opening 2 to 6 openings 7 to 14 openings 15 or more openings	196 sq.in. 324 sq.in. 484 sq.in. 484 sq.in. + 10 sq.in. for each additional opening		Not applicable

1. Area for medium-and high-heat chimneys shall be determined using accepted engineering methods and as approved by the building official.

2. Where fireplaces open on more than one side, the fireplace opening shall be measured along the greatest dimensions.

Note: For altitudes over 2,000 feet (610 m) above sea level, the building official shall be consulted in determining the area of the passageway.

Table No. 31-B Construction, Clearance and Termination Requirements for Masonry and Concrete Chimneys

Chimney Serving	THICKNESS (min. inches) x 25.4 for mm		Height above roof opening (feet) x 304.8 for mm	Height above any part of building within (feet) x 304.8 for mm			Clearance to combustible construction (inches) x 25.4 for mm	
	Wall s	Lining		10	25	50	Int. Inst.	Ext. Inst.
1. RESIDENTIAL-TYPE APPLIANCES[1,2] (low Btu input)			2	2			2	1 or ½ gypsum[5]
Clay, shale or concrete brick	4[3]	5/8 fire-clay tile or 2 firebrick						
Reinforced concrete	4[3]	4½ firebrick						
Hollow masonry units	4[4]							
Stone	12							
Unburned clay units	8							
5. RESIDENTIAL-TYPE INCINERATORS	Same as for residential-type appliances shown above							

1. See Table 9-A of the Mechanical Code for types of appliances allowed with each type of chimney.
2. Lining shall extend from bottom to top of chimney.
3. Chimneys having walls 8 inches (203 mm) or more in thickness may be unlined.
4. Equivalent thickness including grouted cells when grouted solid. The equivalent thickness may also include the grout thickness between the liner and masonry unit.
5. Chimneys for residential-type appliances installed entirely on the exterior of the building. For fireplace and barbecue chimneys, see Section 3102.7.8.

9.2 California Energy Conservation Standards. Mandatory Features and Devices - 1992

Energy Efficiency Standards for Residential and Non-Residential Buildings - Subchapter 7 (Section 150):
Low-Rise Residential Buildings - Mandatory Features and Devices.

Section 150 Mandatory Features and Devices.

(e) Installation of Fireplaces, Decorative Gas Appliance, and Gas Logs.

1. If a masonry or factory-built fireplace is installed, it shall have the following.

A. Closable metal or glass doors covering the entire opening of the firebox;

B. A combustion air intake to draw air from the outside of the building directly into the firebox,, which is at least 6-square inches (3871 sq.mm.) in area and is equipped with a readily accessible, operable, and tight-fitting damper or combustion air control device, and

EXCEPTION to Section 150(e)1.B.: An outside combustion air intake is not required if the fireplace will be installed over concrete slab flooring and the fireplace will not be located on an exterior wall.

C. A flue damper with a readily accessible control.

EXCEPTION to Section 150(e)1.C.: When a gas log, log lighter, or decorative gas appliance is installed in a fireplace, the flue damper shall be blocked open if required by the manufacturer's installation instructions or the State Mechanical Code.

2.   Continuous burning pilot lights and the use of indoor air for cooling a firebox jacket, when that indoor air is vented to the outside of the building, are prohibited.

604-6   MASONRY CHIMNEYS

604-6.1 General

Construct and install chimneys which are structurally safe, durable, smoke-tight and capable of withstanding action of flue gases.

604-6.2 Construction

(a) Masonry chimney walls shall be constructed of masonry units with walls not less than 4 in. (102 mm) thick or rubble stone masonry not less than 12 in. (305 mm) thick. Masonry shall be laid with full, push filled, cross and bed, mortar joints. Concrete masonry shall be solid units.

(b) Chimneys and masonry fireplaces shall be supported on concrete or other masonry. Chimneys shall not support loads other than their own weight unless they are designed and constructed to support the additional load.

(c) Provide a thimble for all masonry chimneys except fireplace chimneys. A cleanout door at the bottom of chimney shall be installed in chimneys serving solid fuel-burning equipment.

(d) Provide a chimney cap of concrete or other waterproof non-combustible material   Chimney cap shall be sloped from flue to outside edge. Minimum thickness of concrete cap at outside edge is 2 in (50.8 mm)

(e) Mortar for flue lining shall be type M or S, be fire clay mortar.

604-6.3 Clearance From Combustible Material

Masonry chimney walls shall be separated from combustible construction as follows

(a) Framing members, 2-inch (50 8 mm) airspace. Airspace shall be fire-stopped at each floor level with strips of asbestos board or other non-combustible material.

(b) Subfloor, flooring and roof sheathing, ¾ inches (19.1 mm) airspace.

(c) Furring strips not wider than 1 ½ inches (38 1 mm), may be installed with zero clearances at corners of chimney

(d) Piers built integrally with chimney for support of wood beams or girders may be used provided wood is separated from the chimney masonry with at least 2-inch (50.8 mm) airspace

604-6.4 Chimney Termination Height

(a) Masonry chimneys shall extend at least 2-feet (.61 m) above any part of a roof or roof ridge or parapet wall within 10-feet (3.05. m) of the chimney.

(b) Except as provided in Div. 615, no chimney shall terminate less than 4-feet (101.6 m) in vertical height above the highest barometric damper or draft hood on connected appliances.

604-6.5 Chimney Connectors

(a) *Metal.* Chimney connectors (smokepipes for appliances using solid or liquid fuels, and vent connectors for gas-fired incinerators, or gas appliances without draft hood, shall be constructed of material having a resistance to corrosion and heat not less than that of No. 24 galvanized sheet metal

(b) *Masonry.* Masonry connectors or breeching shall be made of refractory material equivalent in resistance to heat and corrosion to high duty fire brick (ASTM C-106 Type A) not less than 3 ½ in (88.9 mm) thick.

(c) Chimney connector (smokepipe) shall have a maximum length from appliance outlet to chimney of 10 ft. (3.05 m) or 75 percent of the vertical height of the chimney, whichever is less

604-6.6 Chimney Flue Area

(a) The flue area for an appliance using solid or liquid fuel shall be as recommended by the appliance manufacturer or ad determined by data in the ASHRAE Guide

(b) The area of a chimney into which two or more appliances are connected shall be not less than the area of the largest chimney connector plus 50 percent of the area of all other appliance connectors.

(c) Area of flue serving fireplace shall be not less than the following:

> (1) $\frac{1}{10}$ of area of fireplace opening for chimneys 15-feet (4.6 m) in height or over.
> (2) $\frac{1}{8}$ of area of fireplace opening for chimneys under 15-feet (4 6 m) in height

(3) Corner fireplaces or fireplaces open on two or more sides are considered special and shall be designed for each specific installation.

(4) Height of chimney is measured from fireplace throat to top of chimney.

604-6.7 Flue Lining

(a) Fire-clay flue lining, not less than $^5/_8$ in. (15.9 mm) thick or other equally durable and heat-resistant material, shall be in all masonry chimneys except that flue lining may be omitted in fireplace chimneys only, when chimney walls are at least 8 inches (203 mm) (nominal) in thickness.

(b) Flue linings shall be supported on masonry or concrete and shall extend from a point at least 8 inches (203 mm) below the flue connector to top of chimney; or for fireplaces, from top of throat to top of chimney.

(c) Where two flues adjoin each other in same chimney, stagger joints at least 7 inches (178 mm) or install wythe.

(d) Where more than two flues are located in same chimney, install 4-inch (102 mm) wythe bonded into chimney separating flues into groups of one or two.

(e) Where diagonal offsets are necessary, bevel edges of flue liner at change in direction to insure smooth, tight joints.

(f) Flue lining shall resist without cracking or softening at temperature of 1800°F. (982°C).

604-6.8 Chimney Reinforcing and Anchorage

Where earthquake design is required, masonry chimney shall be reinforced and anchored to frame as follows'

(a) *Vertical Bars*

Chimney area (sq. in.)	No. of Bars	Size of Bars
Less than 300	4	No. 3
300 or over	4	No. 4

(b) *Horizontal Bars*

(1) No. 2 bars, 24 inches (610 mm) o c. embedded in mortar joints and
(2) No. 3 bars at chimney cap and each plane of anchorage

(c) *Anchorage*

(1) Anchor chimneys which are entirely or partly outside of exterior walls to structures at each floor line 6-feet (1.8 m) or more above grade at the upper ceiling or roof line
(2) Anchorage shall consist of ¼-inch (6.4 mm) steel straps or equivalent reinforcing bars anchored to chimney masonry and to structural members of framework.

604-7   MASONRY FIREPLACES

604-7.1 General

Fireplace construction shall be safe, durable and suitable for its intended use   All site-built fireplaces, solid fuel or gas burning, shall be provided with a source of combustion air from outside the conditioned atmosphere of the home, directed (1) into the combustion chamber proper, or (2) into the room and along the same wall close to the appliance   The combustion air supply duct shall be sized for flow of air needed by the appliance independent of infiltration through the structure. Any duct supplying air shall be equipped with screening with not more than ¼ in. (6.4 mm) mesh and a tightly closing damper An operable window in the same room may be considered as a source of air when located to assure draft-free comfort for occupants.

604-7.2 Construction

(a) Fireplaces shall be supported on concrete or other masonry. Concrete masonry shall be solid units

(b) Install damper in accordance with manufacturer's recommendations. Damper shall be of type which will effectively close the flue passage.

(c) Parge smoke chamber with fire-clay mortar (refractory mortar) on all sides. Parging may be omitted if wall thickness is 8 inches (203 mm) Masonry mortar shall not be used for parging.

(d) Hearth, including inner and outer hearth shall be fire brick, brick, concrete, stone, tile or other non-combustible heat-resistant material

(e) Outer hearth shall extend at least 16 inches (406 mm) in front of opening and at least 8 inches (203 mm) each side of fireplace opening. A separate outer hearth is not required when floor construction and finish floorings are of non-combustible materials.

(f) Where a lining of fire brick at least 2 inches (50 8 mm) is provided, the total thickness of firebox wall, including lining, shall not be less than 8 inches (203 mm). Where fire brick lining is not provided thickness shall not be less than 12 inches (305 mm). Steel fireplace lining, at least ¼-inch (6 4 mm) thick, may be used in lieu of fire brick lining. Installation shall be in accordance with manufacturer's recommendations.

(g) Separate flues shall be installed for each fireplace

(h) Masonry over a fireplace opening shall be supported by a lintel on non-combustible material

604-7.3   Clearances from Combustible Construction

(a) Fireplace walls shall be separated from combustible construction as follows:

(1) Framing members, 2-inch (50 8 mm) airspace. Airspace, shall be firestopped at floor level with extension of ceiling finish, strips of asbestos board or other non-combustible material. (*)

(2) Subfloor and flooring ¾-inch (19.1 mm) airspace.

(b) Piers built integrally with fireplace to support wood construction may be used provided wood is separated from fireplace masonry with at least 2-inch (50 8 mm) airspace.

(c) Combustible material shall not be placed within 3½ inch (89 mm) of the edges of a fireplace opening. Combustible material above and projecting more than 1½ inch (38 mm) in front of fireplace opening shall be placed at least 12 inch (305 mm) above opening.

(*)Author's comment—Asbestos board not now permitted—use type X gyp board or Imperial Firecode "C" Gypsum Base)

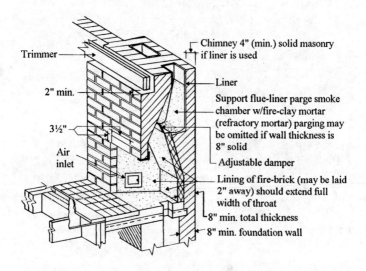

Trimmer

2" min.

3½"

Air inlet

Chimney 4" (min.) solid masonry if liner is used

Liner

Support flue-liner parge smoke chamber w/fire-clay mortar (refractory mortar) parging may be omitted if wall thickness is 8" solid

Adjustable damper

Lining of fire-brick (may be laid 2" away) should extend full width of throat

8" min. total thickness

8" min. foundation wall

Figure 9-1   Cut-away section of typical fireplace

Dampers are used in all fireplaces. They are located in the forward part of the fireplace to allow for a smoke shelf. They should be no less than 6 inches (152 mm) to 8 inches (203 mm) above the top of the fireplace opening. When fully opened, they are required to stand vertically at least ½ inch (12.7 mm) to the room side of the vertical projection of the inner face of the flue. When fully opened, damper openings should be not less than 90% of the required flue area.

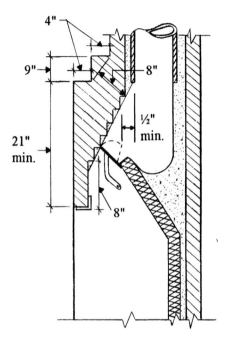

Figure 9-2   Blade damper

Adjacent Flues

Tops of adjacent flues should have a height difference of at least 2 inches (50.8 mm) and may be as much as 12 inches (305 mm) to prevent smoke from pouring from one flue into the other. The fireplace on the upper floor should have the top of its flue higher than the flue of the fireplace on the lower floor.

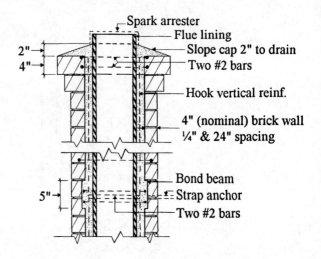

Figure 9-3   Lined chimney

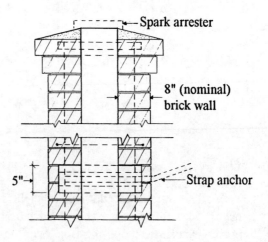

Figure 9-4   Unlined chimney

REINFORCEMENT AND ANCHORAGE IN SEISMIC ZONES 2, 3 and 4.

In Seismic Zones 2, 3 and 4, masonry chimneys in wood frame buildings should be anchored at each floor and roof line more than 6 feet (1.83 m) above grade for a minimum horizontal force of 900 pounds (409 kg) in any direction. Two steel straps secured to chimney vertical reinforcement and fastened to the structural framework of the building in accordance with the illustrations may be considered adequate anchorage, provided the unsupported height of chimney above the top most anchor does not exceed 3 feet (914 mm).

(1) Secure two 1 inch (25.4 mm) steel anchor straps to 2 inch (50.8 mm) by 4 inch (101.6 mm) ties of sufficient length to span 3 ceiling joists with ½ inch (12.7 mm) diameter bolts or with 16d nails.

(2) Additional reinforcement may be required as indicated by engineering analysis.

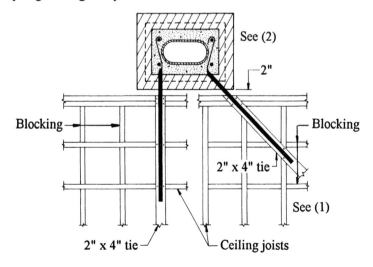

Figure 9-5   Plan at ceiling

Only a few of the many styles of brick chimneys. (London, England)

REFERENCES

1985, 1988, 1991 and 1994 editions of the Uniform Building Code, published by the International Conference of Building Officials, Whittier, California.

ASTM C-315 Flue Lining Installation Standard, 1994.

Book of Successful Fireplaces by R.J. Lytle and Marie-Jeanne Lytle, published by Structures Publishing Company, Farmington, Michigan, 1977.

California Energy Conservation Standards, published by California State Building Code Part 2, Tile 24, 1992.

Canadian Building Digest, Division of Building Research, National Research of Canada, UDC 697.83, by F. Steel, July 1981.

Contemporary Brick Masonry Fireplaces, Technical Notes 19c, Brick Institute of America, Reston, Virginia.

Fireplace Technology In An Energy Conscious World by Harry Morstead, published by Centre for Research and Development in Masonry, Calgary, Alberta, Canada, 1983.

Fireplaces by Ken Kern and Steve Magers, published by Charles Scribner's Sons, New York, 1978.

How to Install a Fireplace by Donald R. Brann, Revised Edition, 1978, published by Directions Simplified, Inc., Briarcliff Manor, New York.

How to Plan and Build Your Fireplace, A Sunset Book, published by Lane Books, Menlo Park, California, 1967.

Ideas for Building Barbecues, A Sunset Book, published by Lane Books, Menlo Park, California, 1970.

Masonry Construction Sep. 91, Damper Basics P. 358-361, Robin Dougherty.

Minimum Property Standards for Housing 4900.1, 4910.1, 4920.1, 4930.1 published by U.S. Department of Housing and Urban Development, 1984.

Planning and Building Your Fireplace by Margaret and Wilbur Eastman, published by Garden Way Publishing, Charlotte, Vermont, 1976.

Recommended Practices for Concrete Masonry Chimney and Fireplace Construction, Tek Spec. No. 3 by New York State Concrete Masonry Assoc., Watertown, New York, 1987.

Residential Fireplace Design, Technical Notes 19, Revised January 1993.

Specifying The Design and Construction of Masonry Fireplaces and Domestic Chimney by David J. Warren and Harry Morstead, published by Centre for Research and Development in Masonry, Calgary, Alberta, Canada, 1983.

Superior Clay Fireplace Catalog, Urichsville, Ohio, 1992.

Superior Fireplace Company Product Catalogues, Fullerton, California, 1985.

The Book of Masonry Stoves by David Lyle, published by Brick House Publishing Co., Inc., Andover, Massachusetts, 1984.

The Collected Works of Count Rumford; Sanford Brown, ed; Harvard Press; 1969; vol. 2.

The Forgotten Art of Building a Good Fireplace by Vrest Orton, published by Yankee, Dublin, New Hampshire, 1969.

The Masonry Fireplace Design Book, published by Northwest Fireplace Association, Seattle, Washington, 1978.

The Open Fireplace; Putnam, J.Pickering; Jas. Osgood & Co.; 1881, Boston, Massachusetts.

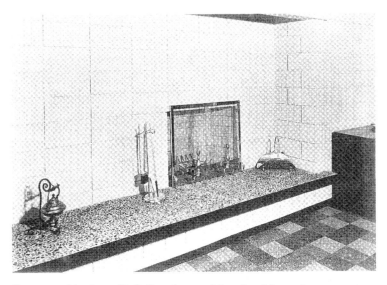

Concrete block wall & fireplace with raised hearth

Interior Barbecue

INDEX

A

B

C

D

E

F

R

S

T

U

V

W